Quechua
PHRASEBOOK & DICTIONARY

Acknowledgments
Publisher Mina Patria
Associate Product Director Angela Tinson
Product Editor Martine Power
Series Designer James Hardy
Language Writer Serafín M Coronel-Molina
Cover Image Researcher Naomi Parker

Thanks
Sasha Baskett, Helvi Cranfield, Anna Harris, Indra Kilfoyle, Chris Love,
Wayne Murphy, John Taufa

Published by Lonely Planet Publications Pty Ltd
ABN 36 005 607 983

4th Edition – October 2014
ISBN 978 1 74321 191 5
Text © Lonely Planet 2014
Cover Image Locals on a bus, Orient/Huber, 4Corners
Printed in China 10 9 8 7 6 5 4 3 2

MIX
Paper from
responsible sources
FSC™ C021741

about the author

Serafín M Coronel-Molina is a native speaker of Quechua from the Peruvian highlands with experience in indigenous language policy and planning, and second language acquisition. He has taught Spanish and Quechua at different times in various institutions in Peru, Mexico and the United States, and taught both languages at the University of Michigan for two years with a joint appointment in the Department of Romance Languages and Literatures, and the Latin American and Caribbean Studies Program. He has a PhD in Educational Linguistics from the University of Pennsylvania in Philadelphia (USA). He has published scholarly articles and presented papers both nationally and internationally relating to indigenous language policy/planning in the Andean region, and Quechua sociolinguistics, including one article written entirely in Quechua about Quechua language planning, and published in the journal Amerindia: Revue d'Ethnolinguistique Amérindienne (vol. 24). The Sustainable Travel section was created by Ozwaldo Munoz and Quentin Frayne.

from the author

No book comes into being without the help and support of many people, and this one is no exception. Thus I would like to gratefully acknowledge the patience and understanding of my wife, Linda Grabner-Coronel, and my daughter Flor de María, when I was so single-mindedly concentrating on the writing of this phrasebook. Even more, I owe my wife a large debt of gratitude for going so far as to stay up late with me many a night to help me proofread the text and keep details consistent throughout the book. I couldn't have done it without her eagle eyes. Annelies Mertens, my editor, is another person whose sharp eyes, linguistic knowledge and editorial skill helped polish the book into publishable form, and I thank her for her patience with my idiosyncratic working style. Finally, to my friend and native Quechua speaker Juan Arroyo, I offer my thanks for a helpful telephone conversation in and about Quechua, when he helped me to judge the comprehensibility of a few phrases I had struggled with. All of these people have contributed to making this phrasebook the useful tool it is. Grateful acknowledgment is made to Rodolfo Cerrón-Palomino/Lingüística Aymara, Lima, Peru: Centro de Estudios Regionales Andinos 'Bartolomé de Las Casas' for use of data from their Quechua language map © 2000.

CONTENTS

quechua

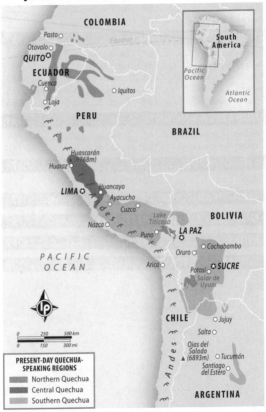

PRESENT-DAY QUECHUA-
SPEAKING REGIONS
- Northern Quechua
- Central Quechua
- Southern Quechua

INTRODUCTION

Travelling in the Andes will be much more enjoyable and worthwhile if you can speak some Quechua, the language of the Incas, also known as *runasimi*, roo·nah·*see*·mee.

Despite the official status of Spanish, which was brought to Latin America by the conquistadors, you'll find that Quechua is spoken in six South American countries: Peru, Bolivia, Ecuador, Colombia, Argentina and Chile. Most Quechua speakers are found in the Andes, although some live in the jungle or on the coast.

Quechua is actually a family of languages that has been spoken by many different peoples in the Andean region long before the Incas began to consolidate their empire in the 13th century AD. The Inca empire reached the height of its development in the 15th century, just 70 years before the arrival of the Spaniards in 1532. The Incas adopted Quechua as their official language in order to facilitate communication with their multilingual subjects.

Today, there are approximately 24 different dialects of Quechua, divided into regional branches known as Northern, Central and Southern Quechua. All these varieties combined are spoken by approximately eight to 10 million people, making Quechua the most widely spoken indigenous language in the Americas.

IN CASE I DON'T SEE YOU ...

The expressions *Wuynus diyas*, *Wuynas tardis* and *Wuynas nuchis*, for 'Good morning', 'Good afternoon' and 'Good evening/night', were borrowed long ago from Spanish and have become much more common than the original Quechua words.

INTRODUCTION

In this phrasebook, we use the Cuzco variety of Quechua, a southern Peruvian dialect (in the Southern Quechua linguistic branch), which is the most widely spoken in the Quechua family. It's well understood in the Peruvian departments of Apurímac, Ayacucho, Cuzco, Huancavelica and Puno, in all of Bolivia, and in the province of Santiago del Estero in Argentina, despite small differences. It can be partially understood in all other Quechua-speaking areas of the Andes, although there are some minor regional variations in pronunciation, word endings and vocabulary. You should be able to get your basic message across with Cuzco Quechua wherever you travel in the Andes.

By speaking some Quechua, you'll break down invisible barriers and show people that you have a genuine interest in their culture and language. Hearing it spoken by foreigners, however haltingly, will be appreciated by native speakers. They'll gain through seeing their language valued by visitors, and your experience will be enhanced through the goodwill shared with them.

ABBREVIATIONS USED IN THIS BOOK

adj	adjective	pl	plural
adv	adverb	prep	preposition
f	feminine	pron	pronoun
inf	infinitive	sg	singular
m	masculine	v	verb
n	noun		

PRONUNCIATION

Quechua is fairly straightforward to pronounce. Beside each word and phrase in this book, you'll find a simple pronunciation guide. It appears in colour and words are divided into syllables with a dot. The Quechua writing system is represented by italic letters.

VOWEL SOUNDS

In spoken Quechua, there are five vowel sounds that correspond to the three basic written vowels *(a, i* and *u)* of the official Quechua writing system, as approved by the Peruvian government in 1985.

Sound	Description	Quechua	
ah	as the 'a' in 'father'	*a*	
ee	as the 'ee' in 'see'	*i, iy*	
e	as the 'e' in 'bet'	*i*	(when found before or after consonants *q, q'* or *qh*)
oo	as the 'oo' in 'hoot'	*u, uw*	
o	as the 'o' in 'got'	*u*	(when found before or after consonants *q, q'* or *qh*)

PRONUNCIATION

Diphthongs

The Quechua writing system combines the letters *w* and *y* with *a*, *i* or *u* to form the following diphthongs (vowel sounds).

Sound	Description	Quechua
ow	as the 'ow' in 'vow'	aw
ai	as the 'ai' in 'aisle'	ay
yoo	as the 'u' in 'union'	iw
ay	as the 'ay' in 'day'	ay (when before or after the consonants q, q' or qh)
ui	as the 'ouie' in 'Louie'	uy
oy	as the 'oy' in 'toy'	uy (when before or after the consonants q, q' or qh)

CONSONANT SOUNDS

Most consonants are pronounced basically as they are in English. A few of the sounds are not common in English, but they shouldn't prove too difficult – the most challenging might be the 'ejective' consonants, explained on page 14.

SAY IT WITH PRIDE

According to some researchers, the term runasimi, roo·nah·*see*·mee, which means 'human speech', was used pejoratively by Spaniards in colonial times to distinguish 'Indian speech' from kastillasimi, kah·stee·lyah·*see*·mee, 'Castilian speech'. Nowadays, this term has lost these connotations and is used with pride by Quechua speakers as a name for their language.

Sound	Description	Quechua
ch	as the 'ch' in 'chew'	ch
f	as the 'f' in 'fun'	ph
g	as the 'g' in 'gun'	g
h	as the 'h' in 'hope'	h
k	as the 'k' in 'skill'	k, q
kh	as the 'ch' in the Scottish loch	k, q, p (at the end of a word)
l	as the 'l' in 'land'	l
ly	as the 'lli' in 'billion' with the middle of the tongue against the roof of the mouth	ll
m	as the 'm' in 'much'	m
n	as the 'n' in 'note'	n
ny	as the 'ny' in 'canyon'	ñ
p	as the 'p' in 'spot'	p
r	like a very short 'd' sound, not like an English 'r'	r
rr	a trilled 'r'	rr
s	as the 's' in 'saw'	s
sh	as the 'sh' in 'short'	sh
t	as the 't' in 'stop'	t
w	as the 'w' in 'wig'	w
y	as the 'y' in 'yes'	y

Aspiration & Ejectives

Aspiration refers to consonants which are pronounced with a small puff of air, as the initial 'p' in the English 'pot' (as opposed to the 'p' in 'spot' – hold your hand in front of your mouth when you say the two words and feel the difference). The meaning of a word can change depending on whether or not a consonant is aspirated. See the box on page 16 for examples of this. In our pronunciation guide, aspiration is indicated with the addition of -h. In written Quechua, aspirated consonants are indicated by the letter *h* after the initial consonant.

Symbol	Sound	Letter
ch-h	as the 'ch-h' in 'Dutch hope'	chh
k-h	as the 'k-h' in 'duck house'	kh, qh
p-h	in the Cuzco area, this sound is similar to an English 'f'; in other areas, the sound is closer to a very soft, breathy 'p'	ph
t-h	as the 't-h' in 'hot house'	th

Ejectives are consonants which are pronounced by stopping the airflow momentarily at the back of the throat and then releasing it. This is similar to the 'tt' in the cockney 'bottle', although other parts of the mouth (the lips, for example) can be used in conjunction with this throat movement to create the ejective sounds which occur in Quechua. Like aspiration, the use of ejective consonants can change the meaning of a word (see the box on page 16). In our pronunciation guide, an ejective is indicated with an apostrophe (') following the initial consonant sound.

PRONUNCIATION

Symbol	Sound	Letter
ch'	sharper and more abrupt than the 'ch' in 'chew'	ch'
k'	made with a click at the back of the throat	k'
p'	made by briefly closing the lips, and then 'popping' or unsticking the lips	p'
q'	made with a click in the throat like the ejective k', but strongly, at the very back of the throat	q'
t'	made with a sharp clicking of the tip of the tongue, a bit like the 'tt' in American English 'button', but more exaggerated	t'

PRONUNCIATION

STRESS

Words are generally stressed on the second last syllable. A stressed syllable in this book is indicated by the use of italics:

| *paqarichiy* | pah·kah·*ree*·chee | to give life/ to establish |

If the word only has two syllables, then it will be the first syllable that's stressed:

| *pallay* | *pah*·lyai | to gather |

An exception to this pattern occurs when an accent is marked over a vowel, indicating that the stress falls on that syllable:

| *¡achakáw!* | ah·chah·*kow*! | Ouch! That's hot! |
| *arí* | ah·*ree* | yes |

PRONUNCIATION

IT'S A BLOW OUT

The pronunciation of aspirated and ejective consonants is one of the defining characteristics of the Cuzco, Puno and Bolivian varieties of Quechua. Be aware that these sounds alter the meaning of words, as these examples show:

chaki	*chah·kee*	foot/leg
ch'aki	*ch'ah·kee*	dry
tanta	*tahn·tah*	gathered together
t'anta	*t'ahn·tah*	bread
thanta	*t-hahn·tah*	old/used/worn out

If you find it difficult to make these distinctions at first, keep trying and it will come. Don't worry too much if you do make a mistake though – your meaning will often be clear from the context.

INTONATION

Intonation patterns in Quechua vary from those of English in one very important way – questions have the same intonation as statements (in Quechua, essentially a falling one). Instead of a rising intonation, specific question words or prefixes indicate that a question is being asked. Quechua also uses a different way of expressing exclamation – the intonation doesn't actually change, instead there is an increased stress on the syllable that emphasises the statement.

This chapter is one of the few overviews of Quechua grammar you'll see. It's not exhaustive, but it will give you enough of a foundation to understand the basic structure of the language so you can construct simple sentences of your own.

In Quechua, sentences are built around basic root words, and the rest of the meaning is added to the sentence by attaching suffixes. In this chapter, to make it easier to distinguish root words from their suffixes, we have used a hyphen between the root and each suffix. The root word always comes first.

There are no irregular verbs in Quechua – all Quechua verbs follow the rules according to each tense. The tenses presented in this phrasebook are the most essential ones.

The following abbreviations are used in this chapter:

adj	adjective	n	noun
assert	assertive	neg	negative
emph	emphatic	obj	object
excl	exclusive 'we'	obl	obligation
fut	future tense	past	past tense
imp	imperative	poss	possessive
incl	inclusive 'we'	pres	present tense
int	interrogative	top	topic
interj	interjection/	uncert	uncertainty
	exclamation	v	verb
lit	literal translation		

WORD ORDER

In general, the basic sentence word order in Quechua is subject-object-verb:

Satuku is eating bread.   *Satuku t'anta-ta-n mikhu-sha-n.*
                          (lit: Satuku bread-obj-assert eating-is)

Note that the assertive suffix indicates that the speaker is stating something from personal experience. See the full explanation on page 22.

Because of the nature of a suffix-based system, word order is quite flexible. You can put any word first to emphasise it:

Satuku is eating *bread*.   *T'anta-ta-n Satuku mikhu-sha-n.*
                            (lit: bread-obj-assert Satuku eating-is)

Here it's 'bread' that's emphasised.

ARTICLES

There's no word for 'the', but 'a/an' is *huq* (literally 'one'). It can also mean 'some' when used with a plural noun:

a restaurant   *huq mikhuna wasi*   (lit: one food house)
some people   *huq runa-kuna*   (lit: one person-pl)

ROOT WORDS

Root words are the building blocks of a sentence, onto which suffixes are attached to create the full meaning.

SUFFIXES

Suffixes do the functional work in a sentence, showing how the various root words work together to give meaning. For instance, *wasi*, 'house', is a noun, but by adding the suffixes *-cha* (which changes certain nouns to verbs) and *-y* (which marks the infinitive), it becomes the verb *wasi-cha-y*, 'to build (a house)'.

Dependent Suffixes

Dependent suffixes can only be used with certain parts of speech or parts of a sentence: they add meaning to a word. An example in English would be the prefix 'un-', as in 'unusual': it cannot be used on its own, but when combined with other words, it carries a distinct meaning (it creates the oposite of the word).

There are three major groups of dependent suffixes:

1. The **nominals** are used only with nouns and pronouns and include the subject marker, object marker, number markers, possessives and several prepositions.

2. The **verbals** are used only with verbs. These include tense, mood and command markers. See Verb page 32.

3. The **derivational suffixes** change one part of speech to another. They have a parallel in English: eg, by adding '-ness', the adjective 'sad' can be turned into the noun 'sadness'. Each specific derivational suffix can only be attached to a specific part of speech, eg, the suffix *-sqa* can only be added to a verb to form an adjective, never to form a noun (see the table below).

to get tired (v)	*sayk'u-y*	tired (adj)	*sayk'u-sqa*
to sit down (v)	*tiya-y*	seat; place to sit (n)	*tiya-na*
head (n)	*uma*	big-headed (adj)	*uma-sapa*
stone (n)	*rumi*	to change to stone (v)	*rumi-ya-y*
little (adj)	*pisi*	scarcity (n)	*pisi-y*
hot (adj)	*rupha*	to burn (v)	*rupha-chi-y*

GRAMMAR

Here are some examples of nominal dependent suffixes, and their uses:

because of/due to/ on behalf of	*-rayku*
I came to Cuzco because of the Inti Raymi Festival.	*Inti Raymi-rayku-n Qusqu-man hamurqa-ni.* (lit: Inti Raymi-because_ of-assert Cuzco-to came-I)
for (the purpose of)	*-paq*
I work for my family.	*Ayllu-y-paq llank'a-ni.* (lit: family-my-for work-I)
from *-manta*	
She/He is returning from Potosí.	*Putusi llaqta-manta kutimu-sha-n.* (lit: Potosí city-from return-ing-she/he)
in (location)	*-pi*
I work in Chinchero.	*Chinchiru-pi llank'a-ni.* (lit: Chinchero-in work-I)
possessive ('s)	*-q/-pa* (after vowel/consonant)
man's	*qhari-q* (lit: man-of)
until *-kama*	
The road goes to Machu Picchu.	*Machu Pikchu-kama ñan ri-sha-n.* (lit: Machu Picchu-until road go-ing-it)
with *-wan*	
They're talking with the police.	*Wardiya-wan rima-sha-nku.* (lit: police-with talk-ing-they)

GRAMMAR

MULTI-FUNCTION SUFFIXES: -TA & -MAN

The suffix *-ta* is can serve numerous functions within a sentence, including:

- object marker, direct and indirect

  I see him.   *Pay-ta qhawa-ni.*
                                (lit: he-obj see-I)

  Can you help me   *¿Yanapa-wanki-man-chu qipiy-ta*
     find my backpack?   *maskhay-ta?*
                                (lit: help-me-could-int
                                    backpack-obj look_for-obj)

  Note that as an indirect object *-ta* can only be used with verbs that don't involve movement of the direct object (see second example). The two verbs – help and find – don't involve movement of the direct object 'backpack'.

- destination, meaning 'to(wards)'

  I'm going to Apurimac.   *Apurimaq-ta ri-sha-ni.*
                                (lit: Apurimac-to go-ing-I)

- derivational suffix, changing adjectives to adverbs

  good   *allin*

  He does well.   *Allin-ta ruwa-n.*
                                (lit: good-adv do-he)

  Here, the two functions of object marker and destination come together in one sentence:

  I want to go   *Apurimaq-ta riy-ta muna-ni.*
     to Apurimac.   (lit: Apurimac-to go-obj want-I)

continues on next page

GRAMMAR

MULTI-FUNCTION SUFFIXES: -TA & -MAN

continues from previous page

The suffix *-man* is similar to *-ta* in that it serves as both an object and destination marker (also meaning 'to(wards)'). Its function as object marker, however, is limited to indirect objects only. It's applied in cases where verbs involving movement are used, and in connection with a concrete noun or the pronoun *pay*.

I give him money.	*Qulqi-ta pay-man qu-ni.* (lit: money-obj he-obj give-I)
to/towards	*-man*
This bus is going to Ecuador.	*Ikwadur suyu-man kay uniwus ri-sha-n.* (lit: Ecuador region-to this bus go-ing-it)

GRAMMAR

Independent Suffixes

The use of independent suffixes is not limited to a particular part of speech. These are attached to the key word in the sentence (which can be any part of speech) but express the speaker's attitude to the whole sentence.

Assertion

The suffix *-n/-mi* (after vowel/consonant respectively) indicates that the speaker is stating something from personal experience.

I speak English.	*Nuqa inlis-ta-n rima-ni.* (lit: I English-obj-assert speak-I)
My stomach hurts.	*Wiksa-y-mi nana-wa-sha-n.* (lit: stomach-my-assert hurt-to_me-ing-it)

Hearsay

The suffix *-s/-si* (after vowel/consonant respectively) indicates that the speaker knows the information second-hand.

People say that village is far away.	*Chay llaqta sinchi karu-s.* (lit: that village very far-hearsay)
People say that she/he speaks Quechua.	*Pay-si runasimi-ta rima-n.* (lit: she/he-hearsay Quechua-obj speak-she/he)

Uncertainty

The suffix *-ch/-cha* (after vowel/consonant) indicates uncertainty over the veracity or validity of words.

He probably speaks Quechua.	*Pay-cha runasimi-ta rima-n.* (lit: he-uncert Quechua-obj speak-he)
There are probably sandals in that store.	*Chay tinda-pi-ch usut'a-kuna ka-n.* (lit: that store-in-uncert sandal- pl there_is-it)

Topic Marker

The suffix *-qa* is an important independent suffix because it marks the repetition of the topic – or main idea or subject – in the conversation. It's therefore referred to as a topic marker.

You don't need to use this suffix the first time you mention a specific subject in a conversation, but after that you must add it to the end of that subject (after all other suffixes, if any exist):

Your brother is sick.	*Turay-ki unqu-shan-mi.*
He can't go to Quito.	*Manan pay-qa Kitu-ta riy-ta* *ati-n-chu.* (lit: brother-your sick-is-assert. no he-top Quito-obj go-to can-he-neg)

Emphasis

The emphatic suffix *-má* is used to express surprise, to correct someone else's statement, to correct oneself, or to simply emphasise a point. It's always the final suffix to be added to a word, and is stressed:

He came all the way from Cochabamba!	*¡Quchapampa-manta-má kuti-rqa-mu-n!* (lit: Cochabamba-from-emph come_back-past-to_here-he!)

Others

Other important independent suffixes are *-chu*, used to mark questions or negatives (see Questions on page 39), *-pis/-pas*, meaning 'and/also/too' (see Conjunctions on page 42) and *-ña*, meaning 'already'.

I already did it.	*Tuku-rqu-ni-ña-n.* (lit: finish-just-I-already-assert)

NOUNS

Nouns are root words (see Root Words, page 18). In general, a noun is expressed as a simple singular entity. If you want to make it plural or modify it in any other way, you do so through the use of specific suffixes.

WE X TWO

It's important to note that, unlike English, Quechua has two categories of the first person plural (we/us). The inclusive category includes the speaker, the listener and anyone else to whom the speaker is referring ('you, me and everyone'). The exclusive category includes the speaker and anyone else to whom she or he is referring, but not the listener ('me and the others, but not you').

GRAMMAR

Plurals

To make plural nouns, simply add the suffix *-kuna*. Note, however, that if a specific number or quantity of something is mentioned, the plural suffix does not need to be added. (See Numbers, page 167, for more on this.)

store	*tinda*
stores	*tinda-kuna* (lit: store-pl)
one boat	*huq wampu* (lit: one boat)
ten boats	*chunka wampu* (lit: ten boat)

Gender

Quechua does not express gender for inanimate objects, only for animals and people. To indicate gender for people, use *warmi*, 'woman', or *qhari*, 'man'. If the gender of an animal is relevant, you have to specifically identify it as *china*, 'female', or *urqu*, 'male'. So a 'female dog' would be *china alqu* and a 'male dog' *urqu alqu*.

Some words borrowed from Spanish explicitly indicate gender, such as *awilu*, 'grandfather', and *awila*, 'grandmother'.

PRONOUNS
Subject Pronouns

Subject pronouns can be expressed with individual words as well as with suffixes. If the context of a sentence makes clear who or what the subject is, the pronoun is not required. The suffixes often provide all the information necessary. These are the individual subject pronouns:

SINGULAR		PLURAL	
I	*nuqa*	we (incl)	*nuqanchis*
		we (excl)	*nuqayku*
you (sg)	*qan*	you (pl)	*qankuna*
she/he	*pay*	they	*paykuna*

GRAMMAR

Subject/Object Pronoun Suffixes

As with just about everything else in Quechua, personal pronouns are expressed through the use of suffixes which identify both the subject and object in a sentence. These suffixes, however, are attached to the verb and are compulsory in the sentence. The pronoun suffixes change depending on verb tense.

I give you money. *Nuqa qulqi-ta qu-yki.*
(lit: I money-obj give-I_
to_ you_sg_obj_pres)

Suffixes for Present Tense

Singular

Subject \ Object	me	you	her/him
I	-	-yki	-
you	-wanki	-	-
she/he	-wan	-sunki	-
we (incl)	-	-	-
we (excl)	-	-ykiku	-
you	-wankichis	-	-
they	-wanku	-sunkiku	-

Plural

Subject \ Object	us (incl)	us (excl)	you	them
I	-	-	-ykichis	-
you	-	-wankiku	-	-
she/he	-wanchis	-wanku	-sunkichis	-
we (incl)	-	-	-	-
we (excl)	-	-	-ykiku	-
you	-	-wankiku	-	-
they	-wanchis	-wanku	-sunkichis	-

GRAMMAR

There's a different suffix for each subject/object combination and for each tense of the verb. Here, the suffix *-yki* indicates the subject, object and tense of the verb at the one time.

I give you (sg) beer.   *Aha-ta qu-yki.*
                                                 (lit: beer-obj give-I_to_
                                                 you_sg_obj_pres)

The following tables show possible subject/object combinations. Some subject/object pronoun combinations are not logically possible in Quechua, so are indicated by empty cells.

Suffixes for Past Tense

Singular

Object / Subject	me	you	her/him
I	-	-rqayki	-
you	-warqanki	-	-
she/he	-warqan	-rqasunki	-
we (incl)	-	-	-
we (excl)	-	-rqaykiku	-
you	-warqankichis	-	-
they	-warqanku	-rqasunkiku	-

Plural

Object / Subject	us (incl)	us (excl)	you	them
I	-	-	-rqaykichis	-
you	-	-warqankiku	-	-
she/he	-warqanchis	-warqanku	-rqasunkichis	-
we (incl)	-	-	-	-
we (excl)	-	-	-rqaykiku	-
you	-	-warqankiku	-	-
they	-warqanchis	-warqanku	-rqasunkichis	-

Note that for the third person (sg/pl) there are no specific object pronoun suffixes. Instead, you'd use the subject pronoun *pay(kuna)* (see page 25) plus the indirect object marker *-man* to express the object 'to him/her/them'. You then add the appropriate subject pronoun suffix to the verb (*-ni* in the example):

Suffixes for Future Tense

Singular

Subject \ Object	me	you	her/him
I	-	-sayki	-
you	-wanki	-	-
she/he	-wanqa	-sunki	-
we (incl)	-	-	-
we (excl)	-	-saykiku	-
you	-wankichis	-	-
they	-wanqaku	-sunkiku	-

Plural

Subject \ Object	us (incl)	us (excl)	you	them
I	-	-	-saykichis	-
you	-	-wankiku	-	-
she/he	-wasunchis	-wanqaku	-sunkichis	-
we (incl)	-	-	-	-
we (excl)	-	-	-saykiku	-
you	-	-wankiku	-	-
they	-wasunchis	-wanqaku	-sunkichis	-

I give them sweets.   *Nuqa misk'i-ta*
paykuna-man qu-ni.
(lit: I sweet-obj them-obj
give-I)

GRAMMAR

ADJECTIVES

Adjectives come before nouns. Only the nouns are pluralised, not the adjectives.

beautiful day	*sumaq p'unchay*	(lit: pretty day)
black donkeys	*yana asnu-kuna*	(lit: black donkey-pl)

Kusi is buying some beautiful clothes.
Kusi sumaq p'achakuna-ta ranti-sha-n.
(lit: Kusi beautiful clothes-obj buy-ing-he)

The concept of 'very' can be indicated by repeating the adjective, as in:

very far away	*karu karu*	(lit: far far)
very big	*hatun hatun*	(lit: big big)

Comparatives

In Quechua, *aswan*, 'more', and *pisi*, 'less', are placed in front of the adjective to make a comparison:

big	*hatun*	
bigger	***aswan** hatun*	(lit: more big)
smaller	***pisi** hatun*	(lit: less big)

It's also very common for either the emphatic suffix *-má* (see page 24) or the assertive suffix *-n/-mi* to be added to the end of the adjective as well:

I'm younger than him.
Pay-manta aswan wayna-má ka-ni.
(lit: she/he-from more young-emph am-I)

Superlatives

The superlative is expressed using 'the most', *lliw-manta aswan ...-n/-mi*, or 'the least', *lliw-manta aswan pisi ...-n/-mi*. The blank is filled in by an adjective:

This town is the biggest.	*Kay llaqta-qa lliw-manta aswan hatun-mi.* (lit: this town-top all-from more big-assert)
That town is the smallest.	*Chay llaqta-qa lliw-manta aswan pisi hatun-mi.* (lit: that town-top all-from more less big-assert)

ADVERBS

Adverbs can be either words derived from adjectives through the use of the adverb marker *-ta* (like adding '-ly' in English), or independent root words. Here are some common adverbs:

easily	*chhalla-lla/phasil-cha-lla*
in this way/manner	*hina*
quickly/rapidly	*usqhay(-lla)*
slowly/carefully	*alli-lla-manta*
very	*ancha/sinchi/nishu*
well	*allin-ta/kusa*

All of the above are 'stand-alone' root words, although some of them carry suffixes to make them adverbs.

GRAMMAR

DEMONSTRATIVES

In Quechua, words like 'this', 'that', 'these' and 'those' can be adjectives when describing a noun, as in *kay qhatu*, 'this market', or pronouns when replacing a noun if it has already been mentioned:

This town is lovely,	*Kay llaqta sumaq-mi,*
that one is not.	*chay-qa manan sumaq-chu.*
	(lit: this town beautiful-assert,
	that-top not beautiful-neg)

There's no difference between singular and plural demonstrative adjectives in Quechua, since it's the noun and not the adjective that is pluralised. Demonstrative pronouns add the suffix *-kuna* to pluralise: eg, *kay-kuna*, literally 'this-plural', thus 'these'.

However, a distinction is made between three – rather than only two – degrees of distance:

this/these	*kay/ankay*
that/those (closer to listener)	*chay/anchay*
that/those (further away	*chaqay/chhaqay/haqay*
from listener and speaker)	

The second form of 'that/those' does not really have an equivalent in English.

This boat is going	*Kay wampu-qa*
to Puno.	*Punu-man-mi ri-sha-n.*
	(lit: this boat-top
	Puno-to-assert go-ing-it)
Those boats over there	*Chaqay wampu-kuna*
are small.	*huch'uy-mi.*
	(lit: that boat-pl small-assert)

GRAMMAR

A BEAUTIFUL DESIRE TO LOVE

Muna-y is a very versatile word, meaning 'to like,' as well as 'to love', 'to desire'; 'to want' and 'to need'. As an adjective, it can mean 'good', 'beautiful' or 'lovely', and as a noun, 'desire' 'love' or 'goodwill'.

POSSESSIVES

Possession in Quechua is shown by adding a possessive suffix to the noun being possessed. You can also add a possessive pronoun when you want to clarify the possession. The possessive pronouns consist of subject pronouns with the suffixes *-q* and *-pa* added (after vowel/consonant). The suffixes are the essential elements for showing possession and are added to the nouns right after the root word, whereas possessive pronouns are mostly used for emphasis.

I just found my backpack.   *Qipi-y-ta tari-rqu-ni-n.*
                             (lit: backpack-my-obj find-
                             just-I-assert)

These skirts are ours.   *Nuqanchis-pa-n kay
                             pullira-kuna-qa.*
                             (lit: ours-assert this skirt-pl-top)

VERBS

Verbs will always have at least one suffix. This obligatory suffix will show what tense (past, present or future) the verb is in, and who or what the subject of the verb is, ie first, second or third person, singular or plural. The suffix *-y* indicates the infinitive of the verb, eg, *ka-y*, 'to be', and this form is used in the dictionaries.

Present Tense

Possessive Pronoun		Possessive Suffix	
nuqa-q	mine	*-y*	my
qan-pa	yours (sg)	*-yki*	your (sg)
pay-pa	hers/his	*-n*	her/his
nuqanchis-pa	ours (incl)	*-nchis*	our (incl)
nuqayku-q	ours (excl)	*-yku*	our (excl)
qankuna-q	yours (pl)	*-ykichis*	your (pl)
paykuna-q	theirs	*-nku*	their

The present tense is used either to indicate an action that occurs once in the present, or to indicate habitual actions. To form it, simply add the appropriate subject pronoun suffix (see Pronoun Suffixes page 26) to the verb root.

Remember that the subject pronoun suffix is essential, but the subject pronoun in parentheses is optional.

I speak Quechua. *Nuqa runasimi-ta rima-ni.*
(lit: I Quechua-obj speak-I)

To express an action that's in the process of happening (like the

Person	Subject Pronoun	Object ('Quechua')	Obj Suffix	Verb Root ('to speak')	Subject Pron Suffix
I	*(Nuqa)*	*runasimi*	*-ta*	*rima*	*-ni*
you (sg)	*(Qan)*				*-nki*
she/he	*(Pay)*				*-n*
we (incl)	*(Nuqanchis)*				*-nchis*
we (excl)	*(Nuqayku)*				*-yku*
you (pl)	*(Qankuna)*				*-nkichis*
they	*(Paykuna)*				*-nku*

'-ing' form in English), insert the suffix *-sha* between the verb root and the subject pronoun suffix:

She's/He's speaking   *Pay runasimi-ta rima-sha-n.*
Quechua.   (lit: she/he Quechua-obj
                      speak-ing-she/he_pres)

Past Tense

To form the past tense, add the suffix *-rqa* in front of the subject pronoun suffix. Note that in the past tense, the suffix *-n* for the third person singular is optional.

Person	Subject Pronoun	Object ('Quechua')	Obj Suffix	Verb Root ('to speak')	Past Suffix	Subject Pron Suffix
I	*(Nuqa)*	*inlis*	*-ta*	*rima*	*-rqa*	*-ni*
you (sg)	*(Qan)*					*-nki*
she/he	*(Pay)*					*(-n)*
we (incl)	*(Nuqanchis)*					*-nchis*
we (excl)	*(Nuqayku)*					*-yku*
you (pl)	*(Qankuna)*					*-nkichis*
they (pl)	*(Paykuna)*					*-nku*

She/He spoke English. *Pay inlis-ta rima-rqa-(n).*
(lit: she/he English-obj speak-past-(she/he_pres))

Future Tense

The future tense is used primarily to express simple future actions ('I'll come tomorrow.'/'Will you come tomorrow?') and probability when used with the 'uncertainty' validator *-ch/-cha* (after vowel/consonant).

In the future tense, most subject pronoun suffixes change form rather than adding yet another suffix to show the tense. Two subject pronoun suffixes, however, remain the same as in the present tense: the singular and plural forms of 'you', *-nki* (sg) and *-nkichis* (pl). When these appear, you'll need to judge by the context whether the speaker refers to the present or the future.

I'll speak Spanish. *Nuqa kastillanu-ta rima-saq.*
(lit: I Spanish-obj speak-I_fut)

Person	Subject Pronoun	Object ('Spanish')	Obj Suffix	Verb Root ('to speak')	Subject Pron Suffix & Future Tense
I	(Nuqa)				-saq
you (sg)	(Qan)				-nki
she/he	(Pay)	kastillanu	-ta	rima	-nqa
we (incl)	(Nuqanchis)				-sunchis
we (excl)	(Nuqayku)				-saqku
you (pl)	(Qankuna)				-nkichis
they	(Paykuna)				-nqaku

They will speak Spanish.　　*Paykuna kastillanu-ta rima-nqaku*.
(lit: they Spanish-obj speak-they_fut)

Imperative

The imperative is a direct command which tells your listener to do something. This is indicated by the suffix *-y*:

Come here!　　　　　　*¡Hamu-y!*
(lit: come-imp)

In the case of a negative command, the sentence begins with *ama* and the suffix *-chu* is added to the verb as the last suffix:

Don't do that!　　　　　*¡Ama chay-ta ruwa-y-chu!*
(lit: don't that-obj do-imp-neg)

(See also Modals, page 37.)

(See also Modals, page 37.)

GRAMMAR

To Be

The verb *ka-y* means 'to be', in the sense of 'to exist', and is also used to describe something or someone, as in *Nuqa turista-n ka-ni,* 'I'm a tourist' (lit: I tourist-assert am-I). *Ka-y* can also mean 'there is/are' when stating something.

Don't confuse the verb *ka-y*, with the demonstrative adjective *kay*, 'this', which has the same spelling (see Demonstratives page 31).

You (sg) are a pretty girl.	*Qan sumaq warma-cha-n ka-nki.* (lit: you-sg beautiful girl-little-assert are-you)
She's/He's on the train.	*Pay trin-pi-n ka-sha-n.* (lit: she/he train-in-assert be-ing-she/he)
We (incl) are tired.	*Nuqanchis sayk'usqa-n ka-nchis.* (lit: we incl tired-assert are-we_incl)
They're in Coricancha.	*Paykuna Qurikancha-pi-n ka-sha-nku.* (lit: they Coricancha-in-assert be-ing-they)
There are a lot of mountains around this town.	*Kay llaqta-pi askha urqu-kuna-n ka-nku.* (lit: this town-in many mountain-pl-assert are-they)

Note that when defining someone or something in the third person, you don't use the verb *ka-y* (or any other verb):

She's/He's a foreigner.	*Pay hawa runa-n.* (lit: she/he outside_ person-assert)
They're healers.	*Paykuna hampiq-mi.* (lit: they healer-assert)

To Have

The verb *ka-y*, 'to be', also serves the function of the English 'to have' in the sense of possession. Literally, it points out something that is or isn't in someone's possession:

Do you have children?	*¿Ka-n-chu wawa-yki?* (lit: there_is-she/he-int child-your)
Yes, I do.	*Arí, ka-n-mi.* (lit: yes there_is-she/he-assert)
No, I don't.	*Mana-n ka-n-chu.* (lit: no-assert there_is-she/ he-neg)
I have a house.	*Wasi-yuq-mi ka-ni.* (lit: house-with-assert am-I)

MODALS

Modals modify the meaning of other verbs in a sentence. They express ability, necessity, desire or need, as in 'can read', 'need to go' and 'want to drink'. As you'd expect, modals also take the form of suffixes.

Must; Should

The simple suffix *-na* plus the appropriate possessive suffix (see Possessives page 32) added to the verb, in that order, indicates the notion of 'must' in Quechua. You can also use the verb *ka-y*, 'to have', which is used only when the obligation implied is unavoidable ('have to') – in which case the progressive form of the present tense *ka-sha-n* (see page 33) is recommended. When the obligation implied is avoidable (eg, 'should' or 'ought to'), the verb *ka-y* is not used.

Must; Have To; Need To

I have to work.	*Llank'a-na-y ka-sha-n.* (lit: work-obl-my be-ing-it)
We (excl) have to leave.	*Lluqsi-na-yku ka-sha-n.* (lit: leave-obl-our be-ing-it)

GRAMMAR

Ought To; Should

I should eat.   *Mikhu-**na**-y.*
(lit: eat-obl-my)

We (incl) ought to rest.   *Sama-**na**-nchis.*
(lit: rest-obl-our_incl)

Can; To be Able

The verb ***ati-y*** meaning 'to be able/to have the ability' is used in a similar way as its English counterpart:

They can dance.   *Paykuna tusu-y-ta **ati**-nku.*
(lit: they dance-inf-obj can-
they_pres)

Must Not; Cannot

Use the negative command form (see Imperatives, page 35). Quechua speakers would typically just say ***Ama chay unu-ta ukyay-chu***, 'Don't drink that water' (lit: don't that water-obj drink-neg).

Like

Muna-y is the verb for 'to like' in Quechua. It can be used by itself or with another verb:

I like Cuzco.   *Nuqa Qusqu-ta **muna**-ni.*
(lit: I Cuzco-obj like-I)

We (excl) like to
buy clothes.   *Nuqayku p'acha-ta
ranti-y-ta **muna**-yku.*
(lit: we clothes-obj
buy-inf-obj like-we_excl)

QUESTIONS
'Yes/No' Questions

To ask a 'yes/no' question, add the independent suffix *-chu* to the most relevant word in the question. Note that the question marker is on the verb:

| Are you (sg) married? | *¿Kasaru-chu ka-nki?* |
| | (lit: married-int are-you_sg) |

The suffix can also be attached to the noun (or to adjectives or adverbs if those are the elements being questioned):

Are you going to	*¿Quchapampa-ta-chu*
Cochabamba?	*ri-sha-nki?*
	(lit: Cochabamba-obj-int
	go-ing-you)

You can answer 'yes/no' questions either with *arí,* 'yes', or *mana,* 'no'. If, in an affirmative answer, you repeat the entire question, the assertive suffix *-n/-mi* (after vowel/consonant) needs to be attached to the most relevant word. When repeating the question in a negative answer, the suffix *-chu* is attached to the most relevant word, while the assertive suffix is attached to the word *mana,* 'no', becoming *mana-n.*

Are you (sg) married?	*¿Kasaru-chu ka-nki?*
	(lit: married-int are-you_sg)
Yes, I'm married.	*Arí, kasaru-n ka-ni.*
	(lit: yes married-assert be-I)
No, I'm not married.	*Mana-n kasaru-chu ka-ni.*
	(lit: no-assert married-neg be-I)

GRAMMAR

Question Words

What?	¿Ima?
What's that?	¿Ima-**taq** chay? ¿Ima-**n** chay?
Who?	¿Pi?
Who's that woman?	¿Pi-**taq** chay warmi?
Whose?	¿Pi-q?
Whose car is that?	¿Pi-q-**taq** chay awtu?
Where?	¿May?
Where are you going? Where are you from?	¿May-ta-**n** ri-sha-nki? ¿May-manta-**n** ka-nki?
Which?	¿Mayqin?
Which market do you like?	¿Mayqin qhatu-ta-**taq** muna-nki?
How?	¿Imayna?
How are you?	¿Imayna-**taq** ka-sha-nki?
How much?/How many?	¿Hayk'a?
How much is that bag, Madam?	¿Hayk'a-**taq** chay waya-qa, mamitáy?
When?	¿Hayk'aq?
When are we going?	¿Hayk'aq-**mi** ripu-ku-sun?
Why?	¿Imarayku?/¿Imanaqtin?/¿Imanasqa?
Why is there no car?	¿Imarayku-**n** mana karru ka-nchu?

Information Questions

With all standard question words, the final suffix *-n/-mi* or *-taq* should be added. If in doubt about endings, use *-taq*.

NEGATIVES

There are two words to express negation. The first one is *mana* (or *mana-n* when asserting something), 'no/not', in conjunction with the negative suffix *-chu*. The second one is *ama*, 'don't', used in negative commands (see Imperatives page 35). Both of them are placed at the beginning of a sentence, while the placement of the suffix *-chu* varies as it's attached to the most relevant word of the sentence.

I don't speak Quechua.	*(Nuqa) mana-n runasimi-ta rima-ni-chu.* (lit: I no-assert Quechua-obj speak-I-neg)
Don't travel alone.	*Ama sapalla-yki puri-y-chu.* (lit: don't alone-you_sg travel-imp-neg)

PREPOSITIONS

Prepositions are expressed through certain dependent suffixes as well as some individual words. For more information, see Suffixes, page 18.

after	*chaymanta/hinaspa/qhipata*
among	*-pura*
because (of)	*-rayku*
during	*-pi*
for	*-paq*
from	*-manta*
in (location)	*-pi*
to/towards	*-man*
until (time/place)	*-kama*
with	*-wan*
without ...	*mana ...-yuq* (used with a noun only)

GRAMMAR

CONJUNCTIONS

Conjunctions are words or phrases that join concepts or parts of sentences.

In Quechua, most conjunctions are individual words rather than suffixes, but there's one exception: *-pis* or *-pas* (used interchangeably) meaning 'also/and/too'. This suffix is added to verbs or nouns as the very last suffix.

You can go to Arequipa by car and by train.	*Karru-wan-**pis** trin-wan-**pis** runa-kuna Arikipa-ta ri-nku.* (lit: car-with-and train-with-and person-pl Arequipa-to go-they)
Me too.	*Nuqa-**pis**.* (lit: I-too)
after(wards)	*chay-qa/chay-man/chay-pa/ qhipa-n-ta*
and/too/also	*-pis/-pas*
because	*-rayku*
but	*icha-qa*
even so/then	*chay-pacha-pas*
finally	*tuku-na-paq-taq/p'uchuka-y-pi*
first (of all)	*ñawpa-q(-ta)*
however	*chay-puwan-pas*
instead	*aswan(-pas)*
nevertheless	*chay-puwan-pas*
next	*chay-qa/chay-man/chay-pa/ qhipa-n-ta*
or	*icha/utaq*
rather	*aswan(-pas)/icha-qa*
so/therefore	*chay-rayku/nis-paqa/chay-mi*

MEETING PEOPLE

When initiating conversations in Quechua, you should be aware that since the time of the Conquest, Spanish speakers have often considered themselves superior to Quechua speakers. One form of discrimination has been a refusal by Spanish speakers to use Quechua at all. If you're in a monolingual Quechua community, there'll be no problem with jumping right in, but if in doubt, try asking in Spanish first:

> Do you speak Quechua?
> *¿Habla usted Quechua?* hah·blah oo·sted *ke*·chwa?

YOU SHOULD KNOW		**YACHANAYKIN**
Yes.	ah·*ree*	*Arí.*
No.	*mah*·nah	*Mana.*
Please.	ah·*lyee*·choo	*Allichu.*
Thank you.	sool·*pai*·kee	*Sulpayki.*

GREETINGS & GOODBYES	**NAPAYKUYKUNAPAS KACHARPARIKUNAPAS**

Greetings and farewells are essential elements of social interaction, and you'll be considered rude if you don't use them. Both greetings and goodbyes should be accompanied by a handshake or a hug. When saying goodbye, a simple wave of the hand is appropriate when you're already at a distance.

Good morning.	*wee·noos dee·ahs*	*Wuynus diyas.*
Good day. (noon)	*ah·lyeen p'oon·chai;*	*Allin p'unchay;*
	ah·lyeen p'oon·chow	*Allin p'unchaw.*
Good afternoon.	*wee·nahs tahr·dis*	*Wuynas tardis.*
Good evening/	*wee·nahs noo·chis;*	*Wuynas nuchis;*
night.	*ah·lyeen too·tah*	*Allin tuta.*
Hello/Hi.	*ree·mai·koo·lyai·kee/*	*Rimaykullayki/*
	nah·pai·koo·lyai·kee	*Napaykullayki.*
Goodbye.	*hokh koo·tee·kah·mah;*	*Huq kutikama;*
	too·pah·nahn·chees·	*Tupananchis·*
	kah·mah	*kama.*
Bye.	*rah·too·kah·mah*	*Ratukama.*

CIVILITIES   YUPAYCHAKUYKUNA

The Quechua people are generally friendly, helpful, respectful people. Reciprocity is a very important feature of good manners in the Andes. If you ask something of someone, you should be willing to offer in return a small gift, like a souvenir from your home country, or a tip.

Please.	*ah·lyee·choo*	*Allichu.*
Thank you	*ah·nyai·chai·kee/*	*Añaychayki/*
(very much).	*sool·pai·kee*	*Sulpayki*
	(ahn·chah·tah)	*(anchata)*
	ah·grah·dee·see·kee	*agradisiyki.*
You're welcome.	*ee·mah·mahn·tah;*	*Imamanta;*
	mah·nah	*Mana*
	ee·mah·mahn·tah·pahs	*imamantapas.*
Excuse me.	*dees·peen·sah·yoo·wai*	*Dispinsayuway.*
Sorry.	*pahm·pah·chah·yoo·wai*	*Pampachayuway.*

FORMS OF ADDRESS

IMAHINA RUNAKUNA NINAKUSQAN

In Quechua, different forms of address represent different degrees of familiarity, or the age of the person being addressed.

As a foreigner in Quechua-speaking territory, the safest form of address for you to use with a Quechua speaker is *Tayta*, tai·*tah*, or *taytáy*, tai·*tai*, 'Sir/Mister' for men, and *Mama*, *mah·mah*, or *mamáy*, mah·*mai*, 'Madam/Mrs' for women, followed by their first name if you know it: *Tayta Satuku* or *Mama Marsilina*.

Madam/Mrs	mah·mah/mah·mai/	Mama/mamáy/
	mah·mah·*lyai*/	mamalláy/
	mah·mee·*tai*/	mamitáy/
	doo·nyah/see·*nyoo*·rah	Duña/Siñura
Sir/Mr	tai·tah/tai·*tai*/	Tayta/taytáy/
	tai·tah·*lyai*/pah·*pai*/	taytalláy/papáy/
	wee·rah·*ko*·chah/	Wiraqucha/
	doon/*see*-nyoor	Dun/Siñur

Note that if you're writing to someone, the forms *Duña, Siñura, Mama* for women and *Dun, Siñur, Tayta* and *Wiraqucha* for men, all have a capital. While *Mama* and *Tayta* must be used with a proper name, *Wiraqucha* can also be used without one. The forms *mamáy, mamalláy, mamitáy, taytáy, taytalláy* and *papáy* are not used with proper names.

FOR THE PEOPLE

Many Quechua speakers call themselves *runa, roo*·nah, which means 'the people'. The Spanish terms *indio/india* (m/f) or *cholo/chola* (m/f) are used by some Latin Americans to refer to the indigenous people. These names are derogatory, so don't use them. Instead, use the Spanish *indígena*, 'indigenous person' or *campesino/campesina* (m/f), meaning 'a farmer/farm labourer; a person living in a rural area'.

MEETING PEOPLE

Miss
to a young woman	*see*·pahs/*p'ahs*·nyah	*sipas/p'asña*
to a girl	see·*pahs*·chah/	*sipascha/*
	p'ahs·*nyah*·chah	*p'asñacha*

young man
to an adolescent	*mahkh*·t'ah	*maqt'a*
to a young boy	mahkh·*t'ah*·chah	*maqt'acha*
little girl/boy	wahr·*mah*·chah	*warmacha*

APOLOGIES

Excuse me. (apology)

pahm·pah·chah·*yoo*·wai/
dees·peen·sah·*yoo*·wai

Excuse me. (to get past)

pah·sai·*koo*·sahkh

It's OK. Never mind.

ah·*lyeen*·mee.
ah·mah lyah·kee·*kui*·choo

PAMPACHAYKUNA

Pampachayuway/
Dispinsayuway.

Pasaykusaq.

Allinmi.
Ama llakikuychu.

HEY YOU!

¡Yaw!, yow!, is an informal way to attract someone's attention, similar to 'Hey!' in English. It's usually combined with someone's name or one of the forms of address we've mentioned. It would be considered rude to use it with an adult, or someone you don't know.

People may call you *ringu/gringu* (m), *reen*·goo/ *green*·goo, 'gringo', or *ringa/gringa* (f), *reen*·gah/ *green*·gah, 'gringa', if they don't know your name. In recent decades in Latin America, these terms have lost their derogatory connotations, and are now terms of respect. If someone knows your name, they might preface it with *Dun/Siñur/Tayta/Wiraqucha* (m) or *Duña/Siñura* (f) – all terms that refer to pale-skinned foreigners.

MEETING PEOPLE

BODY LANGUAGE
ÑAWIWAN, MAKIWAN, UMAWAN RIMAY

Quechua speakers are generally humble and may not look you in the eye when speaking. This is more common in rural areas, where visitors are still rare. In metropolitan areas, where people are familiar with foreign tourists, they're more open and less self-effacing. In tourist areas, as you'd expect, vendors have no hesitation in approaching you with their wares or taking you by the arm to try to convince you to buy something.

¡UPSIDE DOWN, RIGHT SIDE UP!

Many punctuation and spelling conventions used in Spanish have been adopted for use in written Quechua too. Questions *start* with an inverted question mark and end in a normal one; the same goes for exclamations ...!

FIRST ENCOUNTERS
ÑAWPAQ TUPANAKUY

You may find that people may not initiate conversations, or might wait to speak until they're sure that you've finished speaking – but don't hesitate to strike up a conversation, as people are very willing to talk to you once you've shown some interest.

How are you?
   ee·mai·*nah*·lyahn kah·*shahn*·kee?   ¿Imaynallan kashanki?
Fine. And you?
   ah·lyee·*lyahn*·mee. kahn·*ree*?   Allillanmi. ¿Qanrí?
What's your name?
   ee·mahn soo·*tee*·kee?   ¿Iman sutiyki?
My name is ...
   ...·n *soo*·tee   ...-n sutiy.
I'd like to introduce you to ...
   ...·wahn rekh·see·nah·*kui*·chees   ...-wan riqsinakuychis.
I'm pleased to meet you.
   ahn·*chah*·tahn koo·see·*koo*·nee   Anchatan kusikuni
   rekh·sees·*pai*·kee   riqsispayki.

MEETING PEOPLE

MAKING CONVERSATION

IMALLAMANTAPAS RIMAY

Talking about the weather, local food and customs, or asking directions, are always safe openers. Personal questions about age, marital status, income and plans for the day are also perfectly acceptable in Quechua societies. If you're uncomfortable discussing such topics, steer the conversation in another direction, perhaps by answering with a little joke – 'I'm very old', *Sinchi machuñan kani, seen·*chee mah·*choo*·nyahn *kah*·nee, or 'I make enough money to travel once in a while', *Mayninpi purinallaypaqmi qulqita tarini,* mai·*neen*·pee poo·ree·nah·lyai·*pahkh*·mee kol·*ke*·tah tah·*ree*·nee.

Great day, isn't it?
   soo·mahkh p'*oon*·chai,
   ree·kee?

Sumaq p'unchay,
¿riki?

It's cold/hot today, isn't it?
   ahn·*chah*·tah chee·*ree*·shahn/
   roo·p·*hah*·shahn ree·kee?

Anchata chirishan/
ruphashan, ¿riki?

Are you waiting too?
   kahm·pees
   soo·yah·ree·shahn·kee·choo?

¿Qampis
suyarishankichu?

Where are you going?
   mai·*tah*·tahkh ree·*shahn*·kee?

¿Maytataq rishanki?

What are you doing?
   ee·mah·*tah*·tahkh
   ru·wah·*shahn*·kee?

¿Imatataq
ruwashanki?

What's this called?
   ee·*mah*·tahkh *kai*·pah
   soo·teen?

¿Imataq kaypa
sutin?

MEETING PEOPLE

SAY CHEESE & THANK YOU

If you want to take pictures of indigenous people, ask their permission first. It would be considered rude not to offer some little thank-you gift afterwards. In fact, don't be surprised if you're asked outright for some cash!

Can I take a photo (of you)?
    ah·*lyee*·choo p-hoo·*too*·tah   ¿Allichu phututa
    hor·koy·kee·*mahn*·choo?   hurquykimanchu?
Beautiful!
    soo·mahkh!/ah·nyah·*nyow!*   ¡Sumaq!/¡Añañáw!
What a beautiful village this is!
    ee·ma *soo*·makh *lyakh*·ta!   ¡Ima sumaq llaqta!
It's great here.
    ahn·chah ah·*lyeen*·mee   Ancha allinmi
    kai·pee   kaypi.

I'm here ...   ...n *kai*·pee   ...-n kaypi
          kah·*shah*·nee   kashani.
    for a holiday   *how*·kai   hawkay
      (vacation)   pah·chah·*rai*·koo   pacharayku
    on business   lyahn·k'ah·nai·*rai*·koo   llank'anayrayku
    to study   yah·chah·nai·*rai*·koo   yachanayrayku

How long are you here for?
　　hai·k'ahkh·*kah*·mahn
　　kai·pee kahn·kee?

¿Hayk'aqkaman
kaypi kanki?

I'm here for ... weeks/days.
　　no·kah ... see·*mah*·nah/
　　p'*oon*·chai *kai*·pee kah·sahkh

Nuqa ... simana/
p'unchay kaypi kasaq.

We're here for ... weeks/days.
　　no·*kai*·koo ... see·*mah*·nah/
　　p'*oon*·chai *kai*·pee
　　kah·*sahkh*·koo

Nuqayku ... simana/
p'unchay kaypi
kasaqku.

NATIONALITIES

TUKUY RIKCH'AQ
LLAQTAYUQKUNA

You'll find that many country names in Quechua are similar to English.

Where are you from?
　　mai·*mahn*·tahn *kahn*·kee?

¿Maymantan kanki?

I'm from ...	no·kah ...·*mahn*·tah *kah*·nee	*Nuqa ...-manta kani.*
We're from ...	no·*kai*·koo ...·*mahn*·tah *kai*·koo	*Nuqayku ...-manta kayku.*
Australia	ows·*trah*·lyah	*Awstraliya*
Canada	kah·*nah*·dah	*Kanada*
England	een·lah·*tee*·rah	*Inlatira*
Europe	yoo·*roo*·pah	*Yurupa*
India	*een*·dyah	*Indya*
Ireland	eer·*lahn*·dah	*Irlanda*
Japan	*hah*·pun	*Hapun*
New Zealand	*nui*·wah	*Nuywa*
	see·*lahn*·dyah	*Silandya*
Scotland	ees·*koo*·syah	*Iskusya*
the USA	ees·*tah*·doos	*Istadus*
	oo·*nee*·dus	*Unidus*
Wales	*gah*·lees	*Galis*

I live in/by the/a ...	no·kah ...pee tee·yah·nee	Nuqa ...-pi tiyani.
city	lyahkh·tah	llaqta
coast	koos·tah	kusta
countryside	hah·wah·lyahkh·tah	hawallaqta
mountains	or·ko·koo·nah	urqukuna
village	lyahkh·tah	llaqta

CULTURAL DIFFERENCES

SAPAQ YACHASQANCHISKUNA

Andeans are very generous, and if you express appreciation for something in someone's home, like a throw rug, a ceramic piece or some decoration, they might offer it to you as a gift. To avoid causing offence, gratefully accept the offer. The same is true for offers of food and drink.

If you're in a community during a celebration, people will make every effort to get you to participate, especially in activities such as dancing. It's not considered rude to resist such efforts, but be prepared for persistent attempts to involve you!

THE ANDEAN WAVE

If you want to beckon an Andean to you, hold your hand palm out, facing the other person, and waggle your fingers without moving the rest of your arm, as if you were waving goodbye to a child. If you wave your arm from side to side this will be understood as a goodbye gesture, as it generally is in Western cultures.

MEETING PEOPLE

How do you do this
in your country?
 ee·mai·*nah*·tahkh   *¿Imaynataq*
 lyahkh·tai·*kee*·pee *kai*·tah *llaqtaykipi kayta*
 roo·wai·*kee*·chees?   *ruwaykichis?*

Is this a local or national custom?
 wah·keen   *¿Wakin*
 lyahkh·tah·*koo*·nahkh ee·chah *llaqtakunaq icha*
 lyoo lyahkh·tah·*koo*·nahkh *lliw llaqtakunaq*
 kow·sai·neen·*koo*·choo chai? *kawsayninkuchu chay?*

I'm sorry Sir/Madam,
it's not the custom in my country.
 pahm·pah·chai·*koo*·wai *Pampachaykuway*
 tai·*tai*/mah·*mai, mah*·nahn *taytáy/mamáy, manan*
 lyahkh·*tai*·pah *chai*·tah *llaqtaypa chayta*
 kow·sai·*neen*·choo   *kawsayninchu.*

Please don't be offended.
 ah·*lyee*·choo *ah*·mah *Allichu ama*
 p-hee·nyah·*kui*·choo   *phiñakuychu.*

I don't mind watching, but
I'd prefer not to participate.
 k-hah·*wai*·tah   *Qhawayta*
 k-hah·wai·*mahn*·mee, *qhawaymanmi,*
 ee·*chah*·kah *mah*·nahn *ichaqa manan*
 chai·tah roo·*wai*·tah *chayta ruwayta*
 moo·nai·*mahn*·choo   *munaymanchu.*

(But) I'll give it a go.
 (ee·*chah*·kah)   *(Ichaqa)*
 ah·tee·pahs·kah·*lyai*·tah *atipasqallayta*
 roo·wai·*koo*·sahkh   *ruwaykusaq.*

Let's dance!
 too·*soo*·soon!   *¡Tususun!*

I don't know how to dance.
 mah·nahn too·*sui*·tah *Manan tusuyta*
 yah·chah·*nee*·choo   *yachanichu.*

THANKS!

There are two ways to say thank you in Quechua, the traditional *'Sulpáy'*, sool·*pai*, and *'Añay'*, ah·nyai, which is increasingly popular these days.

local	kai lyahkh·*tah*·pee	*kay llaqta*
national	lyoo	*lliw*
	lyahkh·tah·koo·*nah*·pee	*llaqtakunapi*
everybody	*lyah*·pahn/lyah·*pahn*·koo	*llapan/llapanku*

AGE   WATA

How old are you, Sir/Ma'am? (to adult)	*hai*·k'ah wah·tah·*yokh*·mee *kahn*·kee, tai·*tai*/mah·*mai*?	*¿Hayk'a watayuqmi kanki, taytáy/mamáy?*
How old is your child? (to mother)	*hai*·k'ah wah·tah·*yokh*·mee wah·*wai*·kee?	*¿Hayk'a watayuqmi wawayki?*
How old are you? (to child)	*hai*·k'ah wah·tah·chah·*yokh*·mee *kahn*·kee?	*¿Hayk'a watachayuqmi kanki?*
I'm ... years old.	*no*·kah ... wah·tah·*yokh*·mee *kah*·nee	*Nuqa ... watayuqmi kani.*

(See Numbers & Amounts for your age, page 167.)

MEETING PEOPLE

OCCUPATIONS

RUWANAKUNA

What do you do?
ee·*mah*·peen lyahn·*k'ahn*·kee
kai·pee?

*¿Imapin llank'anki
kaypi?*

I'm a/an ...
no·kah ...·n/·mee *kah*·nee

Nuqa ...-n/-mi kani.

aide/assistant	yah·*nah*·pahkh/ yah·nah·*pah*·kokh	*yanapaq/ yanapakuq*
artist	ahr·*tees*·tah	*artista*
businessperson	*rahm*·tekh/k-*hah*·tokh/ teen·*dah*·yokh	*rantiq/qhatuq/ tindayuq*
carpenter	kahr·peen·*tee*·roo	*karpintiru*
chef	*wai*·k'okh/ wai·k'oo·*pah*·kokh	*wayk'uq/ wayk'upakuq*
community leader	kah·*mah*·chekh	*kamachiq*
craftsperson	ahr·tee·*sah*·noo	*artisanu*
dancer	*too*·sokh	*tusuq*
doctor	*dook*·toor	*duktur*
driver	*choo*·feer	*chufir*
engineer	een·hee·*nyee*·roo	*inhiñiru*
farmer	*chahkh*·rah roo·*nah*	*chakra runa*
fisherman	*chahly*·wah hah·p'ekh	*challwa hap'iq*
fortune teller	*wah*·tokh	*watuq*
healer	*hahm*·pekh	*hampiq*
journalist	peer·yoo·*dees*·tah	*piryudista*
labourer	*lyahn*·k'akh	*llank'aq*
lawyer	*yoo*·yai kokh/ ah·woo·*gah*·roo	*yuyay quq/ awugaru*
mayor	ahl·*kahl*·dee	*alkaldi*
mechanic	mee·kah·*nee*·koo	*mikaniku*
minister (pastor)	*roo*·nah mee·chekh	*runa michiq*
nurse	*on*·kokh yah·*nah*·pahkh	*unquq yanapaq*
office worker	oo·fee·see·*nah*·pee *lyahn*·k'akh	*ufisinapi llank'aq*

police officer	wahr·*dee*·yah	*wardiya*
priest	*tai*·tah koo·rah	*tayta kura*
scientist	hah·*mow*·t'ah	*hamawt'a*
shepherd	*mee*·chekh	*michiq*
singer	*tah*·kekh	*takiq*
student	*yah*·chai *moo*·nahkh	*yachay munaq*
teacher	yah·*chah*·chekh	*yachachiq*
university lecturer/ professor	hah·*mow*·t'ah	*hamawt'a*
waiter	mee·*k-hoo*·nah	*mikhuna*
	wah·*see*·pee	*wasipi*
	lyahn·k'ahkh	*llank'aq*
writer	*kel*·kahkh	*qilqaq*

I'm retired.
mah·*nah*·nyahn   *Manañan*
lyahn·k'ah·*nee*·choo,   *llank'anichu,*
sah·mah·koo·*nee*·nyahn   *samakuniñan.*

I'm unemployed.
mah·nah lyahn·k'ai·*nee*·yokh   *Mana llank'ayniyuq*
kah·nee   *kani.*

What are you studying?
ee·*mah*·tahkh   *¿Imatataq*
yah·chah·*shahn*·kee?   *yachashanki?*

I'm studying ...	*no*·kah ....tahn	*Nuqa ...-tan*
	yah·chah·*shah*·nee	*yachashani.*
art	*ahr*·tee	*arti*
arts/humanities	ee·mai·*mah*·nah	*imaymana*
	yoo·yai·*koo*·nah	*yuyaykuna*
engineering	een·hee·nyee·*ree*·yah	*inhiñiriya*
English	*een*·lees	*inlis*
languages	ee·mai·*mah*·nah	*imaymana*
	see·mee·*koo*·nah	*simikuna*
medicine	mee·dee·*see*·nah	*midisina*
science	hah·*moo*·t'ai	*hamut'ay*
Spanish	kahs·tee·*lyah*·noo	*kastillanu*

MEETING PEOPLE

FEELINGS   SINTIMINTUKUNA

If someone asks, 'How are you?', your first response should be a
generic 'I'm well' or 'I'm not well'.

How are you?
  ee·mai·*nah*·lyahn kah·*shahn*·kee?   *¿Imaynallan kashanki?*
I'm well.
  ah·*lyeen*·lyahn kah·*shah*·nee   *Allinllan kashani.*
I'm not so good.
  mah·nahn ah·*lyeen*·choo   *Manan allinchu*
  kah·*shah*·nee   *kashani.*

Are you ...?	...·choo kah·*shahn*·kee?	*¿...-chu kashanki?*
I'm ...	...·n kah·*shah*·nee	*...-n kashani.*
afraid	mahn·*chahs*·kah	*manchasqa*
angry	fee·*nyahs*·kah	*phiñasqa*
depressed	pee·see·*chahs*·kah	*pisichasqa*
grateful	son·kon·chah·*koos*·kah	*sunqunchakusqa*
happy	koo·*sees*·kah	*kusisqa*
in a hurry	ah·poo·*rahs*·kah	*apurasqa*
inspired	kahly·pah·chah·*koos*·kah	*kallpachakusqa*
sad	lyah·*kees*·kah	*llakisqa*
tired	sai·*k'oos*·kah	*sayk'usqa*
worried	lyah·*kees*·kah	*llakisqa*

A phrase such as 'I'm afraid' is easy enough to translate from
English to Quechua, but 'I'm cold' is more problematic. These
feelings require special phrases to express them:

I'm cold.
  chee·ree·wah·*shahn*·mee   *Chiriwashanmi.*
I'm hot.
  roo·p·hah·ree·wah·   *Ruphariwa-*
  shahn·mee   *shanmi.*
I'm hungry.
  yahr·kah·wah·*shahn*·mee   *Yarqawashanmi.*

I'm thirsty.
ch'ah·kee·wah·*shahn*·mee   *Ch'akiwashanmi.*
I'm sleepy.
poo·*nyui*·mee   *Puñuymi*
ai·sah·*wah*·shahn   *aysawashan.*
I'm right. (correct)
rah·soon·nee·*yokh*·mee   *Rasunniyuqmi*
kah·nee   *kani.*
I'm sorry. (condolence)
ahn·*chah*·tahn   *Anchatan*
lyah·kee·*pai*·kee   *llakipayki.*

BREAKING THE   ## RIMANAKUYTA
LANGUAGE BARRIER   ## ATIY

Do you speak ...?   ... ree·mahn·*kee*·choo?   ¿... *rimankichu?*
  English   een·*lees*·tah   *inlista*
  Quechua   roo·nah·see·*mee*·tah   *runasimita*
  Spanish   kahs·tee·lyah·*noo*·tah   *kastillanuta*

Yes, I do.
  ah·*ree,* ree·*mah*·neen   *Arí, rimanin.*
No, I don't.
  mah·nahn, ree·mah·*nee*·choo   *Manan, rimanichu.*
I speak a little bit.
  no·kah pee·see·*lyah*·tah   *Nuqa pisillata*
  ree·*mah*·nee   *rimani.*
Who speaks English here?
  pee·tahkh *kai*·pee   ¿*Pitaq kaypi*
  een·*lees*·tah ree·*mahn?*   *inlista riman?*

MEETING PEOPLE

Do you understand?
    een·teen·deen·*kee*·choo?   *¿Intindinkichu?*

I (don't) understand.
    (mah·nahn)   *(Manan)*
    een·teen·dee·*nee*·choo   *intindinichu.*

Could you speak more slowly?
    ah·lyee·lyah·*mahn*·tah   *¿Allillamanta*
    ree·mai·koon·kee·*mahn*·choo?   *rimaykunkimanchu?*

Could you repeat that?
    yah·pah·*mahn*·tah *chai*·tah   *¿Yapamanta chayta*
    ree·mai·koon·kee·*mahn*·choo?   *rimaykunkimanchu?*

Please write it down.
    ah·*lyee*·choo *kel*·kai   *Allichu qilqay.*

How do you say this in Quechua?
(when pointing to something)
    ee·mah·neen·*chees*·mee   *¿Imaninchismi*
    kai·tah roo·nah·see·*mee*·pee?   *kayta runasimipi?*

What does ... mean?
    ee·mah nee·nahn·*chees*·mee ...?   *¿Ima ninanchismi ...?*

RELIGION   RILIHIYUN

Religion is a topic of everyday conversation – it's certainly not a taboo subject. While the Andean countries are officially Catholic, there's actually a fair amount of freedom of religion. All of the Christian religions are represented, as well as many Eastern religions and beliefs. Names of religions were simply borrowed from Spanish and adapted to the Quechua pronunciation system.

What's your religion?
    ee·*mah*·tahkh   *¿Imataq*
    ree·lee·hee·yun·*nee*·kee?   *rilihiyunniyki?*

I'm (a/an) ...

	*no·*kah ...·n/·mee	*Nuqa* ...*-n/-mi*
	*kah·*nee	*kani.*
Adventist	ahd·ween·*tees·*tah	*adwintista*
Baptist	wow·*tees·*tah	*wawtista*
Buddhist	woo·*dees·*tah	*wudista*
Christian	krees·tee·*yah·*noo	*kristiyanu*
Evangelist	ee·wahn·hee·*lees·*tah	*iwanhilista*
Hindu	een·*doo	*indu*
Jehovah's	ee·wahn·hee·*lees·*tah	*iwanhilista*
Witness		
Jewish	hoo·*dee·*yoo	*hudiyu*
Lutheran	loo·tee·*rah·*noo	*lutiranu*
Methodist	mee·too·*dees·*tah	*mitudista*
Mormon	*moor·*moon	*murmun*
Muslim	moo·*sool·*mahn	*musulman*
Protestant	proo·tees·*tahn·*tee	*prutistanti*

I'm not religious.

*mah·*nah	*Mana*
ree·lee·hee·yoon·nee·*yokh·*mee	*rilihiyunniyuqmi*
*kah·*nee	*kani.*

IT'S THE END OF THE WORD

When using *-n/-mi*, choose the *-n* ending when the preceding root word ends in a vowel, and the *-mi* ending when it ends in a consonant: eg, *adwintista-n*, ahd·ween·*tees·*tahn, or *murmun-mi*, moor·*moon·*mee. Note that using the *-mi* ending will change which syllable is stressed.

COSMOVISION & CATHOLICISM

Catholicism as practised by the indigenous people in the Andes has some intriguing differences from Western Catholicism.

The Andean religion, before the conquistadors introduced Christianity, was more a cosmovision than simply a religion – it was an entire way of viewing the world and explaining natural events. It was animistic, believing that animals and other elements of the natural world have souls. The highest deity was 'Father Sun', *Tayta Inti*, *tai·tah een·tee*, from whom the Incas believed themselves to be directly descended.

Obviously the Incas had great respect for the natural world and its power. Their sacred objects, or *wak'as*, *wah·k'ahs*, were mountain peaks, rivers and lakes, all of whose souls needed to be appeased regularly with ritual offerings, usually of food or drink. *Pachamama*, *pah·chah·mah·mah*, was 'Mother Earth', the nurturing protector and life-giver of all beings, and it was particularly important to pay her for her bounty. This was done through a major celebration that took place every August, known as 'payment to Mother Earth' or *haywakuy*, *hai·wah·kui*. Payments consisted of offerings of coca leaves, food or beverages.

When the Spaniards arrived (1532), they began to convert the locals to Catholicism. The Andeans seemed to accept the teaching of the missionaries fairly readily but, in reality, they did not reject their previous beliefs to accept the new ones. Rather, they syncretised them, or layered

COSMOVISION & CATHOLICISM

them on top of their existing beliefs. The Christian belief in heaven and hell led them to add similar spiritual territories to their organisational schema of the world. In addition to *kay pacha*, kai *pah·chah*, the world in which people dwell, there is *hanaq pacha*, *hah·nahkh pah·chah*, the world above, where the gods dwell, and *ukhu pacha*, *oo·k·hoo pah·chah*, the world below, a world of shadows and darkness. In the Andean cosmology, these three worlds interconnect and their inhabitants interact.

Another example of this syncretism is the Andean belief in God and active worship of the saints. They consider Jesus and the Virgin Mary to belong to this category of saints. Interestingly, they have blended the identities of the Catholic saints with their own *apus*, *ah·poos*, 'principal mountain gods' and *wak'as*, *wah·k'ahs*, 'sacred places'. This was a logical thing to do. For Western Catholics, the saints serve as intermediaries between humans and their God, and in the ancient Andean cosmovision, the *apus* and *wak'as* also served an intermediary function. The Virgin Mary herself came to be associated with *Pachamama*, the Earth Mother, the greatest of all female deities.

The most obvious manifestation of this practice is the habit of putting crosses on mountain tops, and holding traditional festivals on Catholic saints' days, so that the 'Spanish' God and saints and the traditional mountain *apus* and *wak'as* can be worshipped at the same time.

I'm Catholic, but I don't
go to mass.
    kah·too·*lee*·koon *kah*·nee,   *Katulikun kani,*
    mah·*nah*·tahkh   *manataq*
    mee·*sah*·mahn ree·*nee*·choo *misaman rinichu.*
I believe in God.
    tai·tah dee·yoos·*mahn*·mee *Tayta Diyusmanmi*
    ee·*nyee*·nee   *iñini.*
I'm interested in astrology.
    koy·lyoor·koo·nah·*mahn*·tah *Quyllurkunamanta*
    yah·*chai*·tah moo·*nah*·nee *yachayta munani.*

I'm interested in philosophy.
    hah·moo·t'ai·*mahn*·tah   *Hamut'aymanta*
    yah·*chai*·tah moo·*nah*·nee *yachayta munani.*
I'm an atheist.
    mah·nahn dee·*yoos*·mahn   *Manan Diyusman*
    ee·nyee·*nee*·choo   *iñinichu.*
Can I attend this service/mass?
    kai kool·*too*·tah/mee·*sah*·tah *¿Kay kultuta/misata*
    oo·yah·ree·*mahn*·choo?   *uyarimanchu?*
Can I pray here?
    mah·nyah·kui·*mahn*·choo   *¿Mañakuymanchu*
    kai·pee?   *kaypi?*
Where can I pray/worship?
    mai·*pee*·tahkh   *¿Maypitaq*
    yoo·pai·*chai*·mahn?   *yupaychayman?*
Is there a church here?
    kahn·choo een·*lee*·sah *kai*·pee? *¿Kanchu inlisa kaypi?*

ancestor	*nyow*·pah *ai*·lyoo	*ñawpa ayllu*
baptism	oo·*lee*·yai	*uliyay*
christening	wow·*tee*·sai	*wawtisay*
church	een·*lee*·sah;	*inlisa;*
	dee·*yoos*·pah *wah*·seen	*Diyuspa wasin*
cross	koo·roos	*kurus*
deity	dee·*yoos kai*·neen	*Diyus kaynin*
devil	*sahkh*·rah/*soo*·pai	*saqra/supay*
evil spirit	*so*·k'ah	*suq'a*
Father Sun	*tai*·tah *een*·tee	*Tayta Inti*
Festival of the Sun	*een*·tee *rai*·mee	*Inti Raymi*
God	dee·*yoos/yah*·yah	*Diyus/Yaya*
creator	pah·chah·*kah*·mahkh	*Pachakamaq*
of the Earth		
creator	wee·rah·*ko*·chah	*Wiraqucha*
of the Incas		
mountain god	*ah*·poo	*Apu*
secondary	*ow*·kee	*awki*
mountain gods		
Incan priest	*oo*·moo	*umu*
lake	*mah*·mah *ko*·chah	*Mama Qucha*
lightning	ee·*lyah*·pah	*illapa*
mass	*mee*·sah	*misa*
Mother Earth	pah·chah·*mah*·mah	*Pachamama*
Mother Moon	*mah*·mah *kee*·lyah	*Mama Killa*
to pray	mah·*nyah*·kui	*mañakuy*
prayer	mah·*nyah*·kokh	*mañakuq*
priest	*tai*·tah koo·rah; *yah*·yah	*tayta kura; yaya*
procession	proo·*see*·yoon	*prusiyun*
river	*mah*·yoo	*mayu*
sabbath	yoo·pai·*chah*·nah	*yupaychana*
	poon·ch'ai	*punch'ay*
sacred place	*wah*·k'ah	*wak'a*
sacrifice	*hai*·wai	*hayway*

saint (m/f)	tai·*tah*·chah/	*taytacha*/
	mah·*mah*·chah	*mamacha*
shrine	kah·*pee*·lyah	*kapilla*
sin	*hoo*·chah	*hucha*
to sin	hoo·chah·*lyee*·kui	*huchallikuy*
stars	koy·lyoor·*koo*·nah	*quyllurkuna*
temple	*mahn*·ko *wah*·see	*manqu wasi*
Temple of the Sun	ko·ree·*kahn*·chah	*Qurikancha*
thunder	*k-hahkh*·yah	*qhaqya*
witch	*lai*·kah	*layqa*

MAYTAPAS RIY
GETTING AROUND

Arranging journeys by plane, train, bus or taxi is generally done in Spanish or English in the Andean region. In Quechua-speaking communities, such forms of transport are not common – even street signs are usually in Spanish.

Nevertheless, Quechua will be the key to seeking your own way in remote areas, if you need to ask whether a car or bus is available, or which way you should go.

FINDING YOUR WAY

MAYTAPAS RIYTA YACHAY

Excuse me Sir/Madam ...
pahm·pah·chah·*yoo*·wai
tai·tai/mah·*mai* ...

*Pampachayuway
tayta/mamay ...*

Where am I?
mai·peen kah·*shah*·nee?

¿Maypin kashani?

I'm looking for ...
...·tahn mahs·k·hah·*shah*·nee

...-tan maskhashani.

Where's the ...?	mai·*pee*·tahk ...?	*¿Maypitaq ...?*
bus station	oo·*nee*·woos *sah*·yahn	*uniwus sayan*
dock/pier	*wahm*·poo *sah*·yahn	*wampu sayan*
road to ...	...·tah ree·*nah*·pahkh nyahn	*...-ta rinapaq ñan*
train station	treen *sah*·yahn	*trin sayan*

LOCAL TRANSPORT

If you're adventurous, try riding in the back of a pickup truck to get from one place to another. This may be the only way to get off the beaten track. You're exposed to the elements, but it's a great way to see the countryside and get to know the locals. You're expected to offer some sort of payment to the driver, as the Andeans do themselves.

65

What time does the ... leave?	ee·mah oo·*rah*·tahkh ... lyokh·seen?	¿Ima urataq ... lluqsin?
What time does the ... arrive?	ee·mah oo·*rahs*·mee ... chah·*yah*·moon?	¿Ima urasmi ... chayamun?
boat	*wahm*·poo	wampu
bus	oo·*nee*·woos	uniwus
minibus	oo·nee·*woos*·chah/ *meek*·roo	uniwuscha/ mikru
train	treen	trin

How do we get to ...?
ee·mai·*nah*·tahkh ....·man   ¿Imaynataq ...-man
chah·*yahn*·chees?   chayanchis?

Is it close by?
sees·*pah*·choo?   ¿Sispachu?

Can we walk there?
chah·kee·*lyah*·wahn   ¿Chakillawan
ree·koo·*mahn*·choo *chai*·mahn?   riykumanchu chayman?

Can you show me (on the map)?
(mah·*pah*·pee)   (Mapapi)
k·hah·wai·kah·chee·   ¿Qhawaykachi-
wahn·kee·*mahn*·choo?   wankimanchu?

BUT HOW WILL IT END?

Remember, when adding suffixes to words, choose the *first* ending when the root word ends in a vowel, and the *second* ending when it ends in a consonant.

What's the name of this ...?	ee·*mah*·tahkh kai ....·kh/·pah *soo*·teen?	¿Imataq kay ...-q/-pa sutin?
city/village	*lyahkh*·tah	llaqta
highway	*pees*·tah	pista
path	nyahn	ñan
road	kah·ree·*tee*·rah	karitira
street	*kah*·lyee	kalli

DIRECTIONS

Straight ahead.
  syookh/dee·*ree*·choo
To the left/right.
  lyoo·*k'ee*·mahn/pah·*nyah*·mahn
Turn at the next corner/street.
  hah·mokh k'oo·*choo*·pee/
  kah·*lyee*·pee moo·*yui*·kui

YACHACHIYKUNA

Siwk/Dirichu.

Lluq'iman/Pañaman.

*Hamuq k'uchupi/
kallipi muyuykuy.*

across (from)	cheem·*pah*·pee	*chimpapi*
behind	k-*he*·pah	*qhipa*
far	*kah*·roo	*karu*
here	*kai*·pee	*kaypi*
in front (of)	nyow·*pahkh*·pee	*ñawpaqpi*
near	*sees*·pah	*sispa*
there	chai·pee/chai·*nekh*·pee/	*chaypi/chayniqpi/*
	hah·*kai*·pee	*haqaypi*

north	*wee·chai*	*wichay*
south	*oo·rai*	*uray*
east	*een·tekh lyokh·see·nahn*	*intiq lluqsinan*
west	*een·tekh cheen·kah·nahn*	*intiq chinkanan*

Thank you for showing us the way.

sool·*pai nyahn*·tah
rekh·see·chee·*moo*·wahs
kai·kee·koo·*mahn*·tah

*Sulpáy ñanta
riqsichimuwa-
sqaykikumanta.*

For more instructions, see Taxi, below.

ADDRESSES   DIRIKSIYUNKUNA

Addresses are generally indicated in Spanish rather than in Quechua. A typical address might look like this:

> Sra. María Condori Guzmán
> Avenida Tullomayo 428
> Cuzco, Peru

Large cities, such as Lima, La Paz and Quito, may have several postal codes, but this is not common. Post office boxes *(apartado* or *casilla* in Spanish) are popular too:

> Sr. José Huamán Mamani
> Apartado Postal 477 (or Casilla Postal 477)
> Cochabamba, Bolivia

TAXI   TAKSI

Taxis are not widely available in the more rural Quechua-speaking areas. To hold a licence, the driver must speak Spanish, so arrangements are generally made in Spanish – or possibly in English in larger cities.

There are two kinds of taxis. A *taxi oficial* is a state-regulated taxi, which is more likely (but not guaranteed) to have a meter; a *taxi particular* is an informal, privately owned taxi – fares are negotiable. You can flag down either sort in large cities.

Make sure you bargain and settle on a price to your destination before getting in. Taxis are generally inexpensive, but some drivers will raise their prices when dealing with a foreigner. See Bargaining, page 127, for more on this.

Sir/Madam, I want to go to ...
    tai·*tai*/mah·*mai* ...·tah
    ree·tah moo·*nah*·nee
                   Taytáy/Mamáy ...-ta
                   riyta munani.

How much is it to go to ...?
    hai·k'ahn kwees·tahn ...·tah
    ree·*nah*·pahkh?
                   ¿Hayk'an kwistan ...-ta
                   rinapaq?

How much is the ticket/fare?
    hai·k'ahn kwees·tahn pah·*sah*·hee?
                   ¿Hayk'an kwistan pasahi?

Instructions

Yachachiykuna

Please take me to ...
    ah·*lyee*·choo ...·tah ah·*pah*·wai
    Allichu ...-ta apaway.

Keep going straight!
    syookh!
    ¡Siwk!

The next street to the left/right.
    hah·mokh kah·*lyee*·pee
    pah·*nyah*·mahn/lyo·*k'e*·mahn
    moo·*yui*·kui
    Hamuq kallipi
    pañaman/lluq'iman
    muyuykuy.

Please slow down.
    ah·*lyee*·choo
    ah·lyee·lyah·*mahn*·tah ree
    Allichu
    allillamanta riy.

Please wait here.
    ah·*lyee*·choo kai·pee soo·yai
    Allichu kaypi suyay.

Stop here!
    sah·yai *kai*·pee!
    ¡Sayay kaypi!

Stop at the corner!
    chai k'hoo·*choo*·pee *sah*·yai!
    ¡Chay k'uchupi sayay!

GETTING AROUND

BUYING TICKETS   WULITUKUNATA RANTIY

Haggling is common when buying tickets for travel. You can even bargain with a travel agent, but purchasing directly from a bus or train station means paying the posted price. Foreigners will often pay more than locals do, especially in tourist areas. See Bargaining, page 127, for more on this.

Buying tickets at bus stations is usually done in Spanish. Flight arrangements are always made in Spanish or in English.

Where can I buy a ticket?
   mai·*pee*·tahkh   *¿Maypitaq*
   woo·lee·*too*·tah   *wulituta*
   rahn·tee·*rui*·mahn?   *rantirquyman?*
How much is the ticket/fare?
   *hai·*k'ahn *kwees*·tahn   *¿Hayk'an kwistan*
   pah·*sah*·hee?   *pasahi?*
How long does it take to get to ...?
   *hai·*k'ah oo·rah·*pee*·tahkh   *¿Hayk'a urapitaq*
   ...·mahn chah·*yahn*·chees?   *...-man chayanchis?*

BUS & CAR   UNIWUS, KARRU

Bus services come in a wide range of quality and service levels, and once again, transactions are conducted almost exclusively in Spanish. However, you might want to inform yourself on local bus services – or the availability of a car where there are no buses – by asking local Quechua speakers.

What time does the ... bus arrive?	*ee*·mah oo·*rah*·tahkh ... oo·nee·*woos*·kah chah·*yah*·moon?	*¿Ima urataq* *... uniwusqa* *chayamun?*
What time does the ... car leave?	*ee*·mah oo·*rah*·tahkh ... kah·*rroo*·kah *lyok*·seen?	*¿Ima urataq* *... karruqa lluqsin?*
first	*nyow*·pahkh	*ñawpaq*
last	*k·he*·pah	*qhipa*
next	*hah*·mokh	*hamuq*

GOING MY WAY?

In rural areas where there's little or no public transport available, cars often double as buses. Drivers will be on the lookout for anyone going in the same direction. You'll need to agree on a price before accepting the lift – see Taxi and Buying Tickets (pages 68, 70).

Does this bus/car go to ...?
kai oo·*nee*·woos/*kah*·rroo
...·mahn *reen*·choo?

¿Kay uniwus/karru
...-man rinchu?

How many times a day
do buses/cars pass by here?
hai·k'ah *koo*·teen
oo·nee·woos·*koo*·nah/
kah·rroo·*koo*·nah kai·pee
pah·sahn *sah*·pah p'oon·chai?

¿Hayk'a kutin
uniwuskuna/
karrukuna kaypi
pasan sapa p'unchay?

Where does this bus/car go?
mai·tahn/mai·*mahn*·mee
kai oo·*nee*·woos/*kah*·rroo reen?

¿Maytan/maymanmi
kay uniwus/karru rin?

Where's the bus/car stop?
mai·*pee*·tahkh oo·*nee*·woos/
kah·rroo *sah*·yahn?

¿Maypitaq uniwus/
karru sayan?

Which bus/car goes to ...?
mai·ken oo·nee·*woos*·tahkh/
kah·*rroo*·tahkh ...·mahn reen?

¿Mayqin uniwustaq/
karrutaq ...-man rin?

Where can I catch the bus/car to ...?
mai·*pee*·tahkh ...·mahn
ree·*nai*·pahkh oo·nee·*woos*·tah/
kah·rroo·tah hah·p'ee·*rui*·mahn?

¿Maypitaq ...-man
rinaypaq uniwusta/
karruta hap'irquyman?

This is my seat.
tee·yah·*nai*·mee kai·kah

Tiyanaymi kayqa.

GETTING AROUND

Could you let me know
when we get to ...?
    ah·*lyee*·choo ...·mahn   *¿Allichu ...-man*
    chah·yahkh·*teen*·chees   *chayaqtinchis*
    wee·lyai·koo·wahn·   *willaykuwan-*
    kee·*mahn*·choo?   *kimanchu?*

Can you tell the driver to stop?
    ah·*lyee*·choo *sah*·yai   *¿Allichu sayay*
    neen·kee·*mahn*·choo   *ninkimanchu*
    choo·feer·*tah*·kah?   *chuphirtaqa?*

I'd like to get off here.
    kai·pee oo·rai·*kui*·tahn   *Kaypi uraykuytan*
    moo·*nah*·nee   *munani.*

THE FUN BUS

When travelling on local buses and minibuses, be
prepared for an extraordinary acoustic treat and
flexible ideas on what constitutes safe driving. Between
passengers yelling at the conductor, the conductor yelling
out the stops as they come up, and the driver yelling
out the window at other drivers, things can get loud.
There may be music blasting out through numerous
speakers. Local performers might climb on to give an
impromptu performance complete with expectations of
tips, while local vendors tout their wares. Buses are often
overcrowded, especially when animals and food products
are on board.

TRAIN   TRIN

Trains don't run nearly as frequently as buses, but they're generally more comfortable for long-distance travel.

What's the name of this station?
ee·*mah*·tahkh kai   ¿*Imataq kay*
sah·*yah*·nahkh *soo*·teen?   *sayanaq sutin?*
What's the name of the next station?
ee·*mah*·tahkh *hah*·mokh   ¿*Imataq hamuq*
sah·*yah*·nahkh *soo*·teen?   *sayanaq sutin?*
Does this train stop at (Arequipa)?
(ah·ree·kee·*pah*·pee)   ¿(*Arikipapi*)
sah·*yahn*·choo kai *treen*·kah?   *sayanchu kay trinqa?*
There's no train today.
mah·nan treen *kahn*·choo   *Manan trin kanchu*
koo·nahn *p'oon*·chai   *kunan p'unchay.*
Can I sit here?
tee·yai·*mahn*·choo *kai*·pee?   ¿*Tiyaymanchu kaypi?*
I want to get off at ...
...·pee oo·rai·*kui*·tah   ...·*pi uraykuyta*
moo·*nah*·nee   *munani.*

BOAT   WAMPU

Boat travel in the Andes might be by canoe for travelling along rivers and other waterways, or by motor boat or hovercraft when travelling from island to island on large lakes such as Titicaca. Even luxury cruise ships, *hatun wampu*, *hah*·toon *wahm*·poo, are an option, for those wanting to visit the Galapagos Islands.

Arrangements for this type of transport are usually made through travel agencies, although you may also be able to negotiate on the spot.

Where can I find a boat that
goes to ...?
mai·*pee*·tahkh wahm·*poo*·tah   ¿*Maypitaq wamputa*
tah·ree·*rui*·mahn ...·tah   *tarirquyman ...-ta*
ree·*nai*·pahkh?   *rinaypaq?*

Where does that boat go?
    mai-*tah*-tahkh/mai-*mahn*-tahkh   ¿Maytataq/Maymantaq
    chai *wahm*-poo reen?   chay wampu rin?
Where does the boat leave from?
    mai-mahn-*tah*-tahkh   ¿Maymantaq
    wahm-poo lyokh-seen?   wampu lluqsin?
What time does the boat arrive/leave?
    ee-mah oo-*rahs*-mee *wahm*-poo   ¿Ima urasmi wampu
    chah-*yah*-moon/lyokh-seen?   chayamun/lluqsin?

DRIVING   KARRU

Car rentals are generally only available in major cities. If you
decide to rent a car, services – from filling up to repairs – will be
handled in Spanish.

In the larger cities and tourist areas, motorcycling is also
possible. Organised tours are the easiest, but renting or buying
your own motorcycle is an option.

Is there a mechanic around here?
    kahn-choo mee-kah-*nee*-koo   ¿Kanchu mikaniku
    kai-pee?   kaypi?
Is there a gas/petrol station nearby?
    gree-foo *kahn*-choo kai-pee?   ¿Griphu kanchu kaypi?
Where can I buy gas/petrol?
    mai-peen gah-soo-lee-*nah*-tah   ¿Maypin gasulinata
    rahn-tee-*rui*-mahn?   rantirquyman?
Does this road/highway/path
lead to ...?
    kai kah-ree-*tee*-rah/*pees*-tah/nyahn   ¿Kay karitira/pista/ñan
    ...-*mahn*-choo reen?   ...-manchu rin?
How can I go to ...?
    ee-*mai*-nahn ...-mahn   ¿Imaynan ...-man
    ree-mahn?   riyman?
Which is the way to ...?
    mai-*neen*-tahn ...-mahn reen?   ¿Maynintan ...-man rin?
I'm lost.
    cheen-kai cheen-*kai*-lyah   Chinkay chinkaylla
    poo-ree-*koo*-nee   purikuni.

My car has broken down.
  kah·*rrui*·kah *mah*·nahn
  poo·*ree*·tah ah·*teen*·choo

*Karruyqa manan
puriyta atinchu.*

Is there a car here going to ...?
  kah·rroo *kahn*·choo *kai*·pee
  ...·mahn ree·*nah*·pahkh?

*¿Karru kanchu kaypi
...-man rinapaq?*

Where are you going?
  mai·tahn ree·*shahn*·kee?

¿Maytan rishanki?

I'm going to ...
  ...·tahn ree·*shah*·nee

...-tan rishani.

Can you take me there in your car?
  pahkh·tah kah·rrui·*kee*·pee
  ah·pah·wahn·*kee*·mahn
  chai·mahn?

*¿Paqta karruykipi
apawankiman
chayman?*

How much do I owe you?
  hai·k'ah·*tah*·tahkh
  mah·*noo*·*kui*·kee?

*¿Hayk'atataq
manukuyki?*

BICYCLE   WISIKILITA

Mountain biking is, for obvious reasons, one of the most
popular forms of cycling in the Andes. Bicycles are available to
rent or buy in larger cities and tourist areas.

Is ... within cycling distance?
  wee·see·kee·lee·*tah*·wahn
  ree·rui·*mahn*·choo ...·mahn?

*¿Wisikilitawan
rirquymanchu ...-man?*

Is there a bike path?
  kahn·choo wee·see·kee·*lee*·tah
  nyahn?

*¿Kanchu wisikilita
ñan?*

GETTING AROUND

Who can show me the bicycle paths?
pee·tahkh wee·see·kee·*lee*·tah
nyahn·koo·*nah*·tah
rekh·see·chee·*wahn*·mahn?
¿Pitaq wisikilita
ñankunata
riqsichiwanman?

Where can I hire a bicycle?
mai·*pee*·tahkh
wee·see·kee·lee·*tah*·tah
ahl·kee·lai·*rui*·man?
¿Maypitaq
wisikilitata
alkilarquyman?

How much is it per hour/day?
hai·*k'ah*·tahkh *kwees*·tahn
sah·pah oo·rah/*p'oon*·chai?
¿Hayk'ataq kwistan
sapa ura/p'unchay?

Where can I buy a bike?
mai·*pee*·tahkh
wee·see·kee·lee·*tah*·tah
rahn·tee·*rui*·mahn?
¿Maypitaq
wisikilitata
rantirquyman?

I have a flat tyre.
wee·see·kee·lee·*tai*·pah
lyahn·*tahn*·mee t'o·*ko*·ron
Wisikilitaypa llantanmi
t'uqurqun.

Could you help me please?
ah·*lyee*·choo
yah·nah·pah·yoo·wahn·
kee·*mahn*·choo?
¿Allichu
yanapayuwa-
nkimanchu?

bicycle	wee·see·kee·*lee*·tah	*wisikilita*
puncture	*t'o*·ko	*t'uqu*
seat	tee·*yah*·nah	*tiyana*
tyre(s)	lyahn·tah(*koo*·nah)	*llanta(kuna)*

QURPACHANA
ACCOMMODATION

Accommodation choices range from luxury hotels in the larger cities and popular tourist towns, to a humble sleeping space with a rural Andean family. In the smaller communities, a few words of Quechua might be the secret to a comfortable night's sleep.

FINDING ACCOMMODATION		QURPACHANATA MASKHAY
I'm looking for (a) ...	...·tah mahs·k-hah·*shah*·nee	...-*ta maskhashani.*
accommodation	kor·pah·*chah*·nah	*qurpachana*
camping ground	*kahr*·pah roo·wah·*nah*·pahkh *pahm*·pah	*karpa ruwanapaq pampa*
boarding house/ hotel	kor·pah *wah*·see	*qurpa wasi*
Where's a/the ... hotel?	mai·*pee*·tahkh ... kor·pah *wah*·see kahn?	¿*Maypitaq* ... *qurpa wasi kan?*
best	lyoo·*mahn*·tah *ahn*·chah soo·mahkh	*lliwmanta ancha sumaq*
cheap	*mah*·nah chah·*nee*·yohkh	*mana chaniyuq*
cheapest	lyoo·*mahn*·tah *pee*·see chah·*nee*·yohk	*lliwmanta pisi chaniyuq*
clean	pee·*chahs*·kah	*pichasqa*
good	*ah*·lyeen	*allin*

ACCOMMODATION

Is there a hotel here?
kahn·choo *kor*·pah
wah·see *kai*·pee?

¿Kanchu qurpa
wasi kaypi?

Is that a good hotel?
ah·lyeen *kor*·pah
wah·*see*·choo *chai*·kah?

¿Allin qurpa
wasichu chayqa?

Is that a clean hotel?
lui·*loo*·choo chai *kor*·pah
wah·*see*·kah?

¿Luyluchu chay qurpa
wasiqa?

Is that hotel nearby/far?
sees·pah·lyah·*pee*·choo/
kah·roo·*pee*·choo *kah*·shahn
chai *kor*·pah wah·*see*·kah?

¿Sispallapichu/
Karupichu kashan
chay qurpa wasiqa?

Could you show me
that hotel, please?
rekh·see·chee·wahn·kee·
mahn·choo chai *kor*·pah
wah·see·*tah*·kah?

¿Riqsichiwanki-
manchu chay qurpa
wasitaqa?

REQUESTS & QUERIES

MAÑAKUYKUNAPAS TAPUYKUNAPAS

Where can I sleep?
mai·*pee*·tahkh poo·*nyoo*·man?

¿Maypitaq puñuyman?

Is there a toilet here?
kahn·choo hees·p'ah·*koo*·nah/
ees·koo·*sah*·roo *kai*·pee?

¿Kanchu hisp'akuna/
iskusaru kaypi?

Where can I take a bath?
mai·*pee*·tahkh
ahr·mah·*kui*·mahn?

¿Maypitaq
armakuyman?

WATER ...

There are two different words for 'water': *unu*,
oo·noo, and *yaku, yah·*koo. The latter is used
throughout the Andes.

Is there water to wash myself?
kahn·choo *oo*·noo/*yah*·koo
mahkh·ch·hee·koo·*nai*·pahkh?

¿*Kanchu unu/yaku
maqchhikunaypaq?*

Is there water to wash my face?
kahn·choo *oo*·noo/*yah*·koo
oo·p·hah·koo·*nai*·pahkh?

¿*Kanchu unu/yaku
uphakunaypaq?*

Could you please heat up
some water for me?
ah·*lyee*·choo oo·*noo*·tah/
yah·*koo*·tah
k'o·nyee·chee·poo·wahn·
kee·*mahn*·choo?

¿*Allichu unuta/
yakuta
q'uñichipuwa-
nkimanchu?*

Where can I wash my clothes?
mai·*pee*·tahkh
p'ah·chai·koo·*nah*·tah
t'ahkh·sah·*rui*·mahn?

¿*Maypitaq
p'achaykunata
t'aqsarquyman?*

Where's the river/spring?
mai·*pee*·tahkh *mah*·yoo/
pookh·yoo kahn?

¿*Maypitaq mayu/
pukyu kan?*

Where can I find drinking water?
mai·*pee*·tahkh ook·*yah*·nah
oo·*noo*·tah tah·ree·*rui*·mahn?

¿*Maypitaq ukyana
unuta tarirquyman?*

Is there clean water here?
kahn·choo *ch'oo*·yah *oo*·noo/
yah·koo *kai*·pee?

¿*Kanchu ch'uya unu/
yaku kaypi?*

ACCOMMODATION

AROUND THE HOME

Remember that Andean houses may not have the luxury of running water or indoor toilets. Be sure to bring all of your own toiletries, and simply ask for a tub for washing.

At meal times, your host family will expect you to share in their food and conversation, and to try the different dishes on offer.

That was delicious!
soo·mahkh mee·*k·hoo*·nah!   ¡*Sumaq mikhuna!*

ACCOMMODATION

Is there anything to drink?
    kahn·choo oo·kyah·*nah*·pahkh
    ee·mah·*lyah*·pahs?

¿Kanchu ukyanapaq imallapas?

May I have some herbal tea?
    pahkh·tah *ko*·rah
    oo·*noo*·tah/yah·*koo*·tah
    ko·wahn·*kee*·mahn?

¿Paqta qura unuta/yakuta quwankiman?

Is there anything to eat?
    kahn·choo mee·k·hoo·*nah*·pahkh
    ee·mah·*lyah*·pahs?

¿Kanchu mikhunapaq imallapas?

What time do you want us to get up?
    ee·mah oo·*rahs*·mee
    hah·tah·ree·*koo*·mahn?

¿Ima urasmi hatariykuman?

Can I help you with something?
    pahkh·tah ee·mah·lyah·*tah*·pees
    yah·nah·pai·*kee*·mahn?

¿Paqta imallatapis yanapaykiman?

Can I leave my backpack here
until tonight/tomorrow?
    sah·ke·*mahn*·choo
    too·tah·*kah*·mah/
    pah·kah·reen·*kah*·mah
    k'e·*pee*·tah *kai*·pee?

¿Saqiymanchu tutakama/ paqarinkama q'ipiyta kaypi?

May I leave my luggage
here with you?
    pahkh·tah mah·lee·*tai*·tah
    sah·ke·yoo·kui·*kee*·mahn?

¿Paqta malitayta saqiyukuykiman?

Could you lend   *pahkh*·tah ....·tah
me (a) ...?   mah·nyah·wahn·
                  kee·mahn?

¿Paqta ...-ta mañawan- nkiman?

    blanket   *kah*·tah/free·*sah*·rah   *qata/phrisara*
    bucket   *bahl*·dee   *baldi*
    wash basin   poo·*roo*·nyah   *puruña*

COMPLAINTS   PIÑARIKUY

It's very ...	*ahn·*chah *...·*n	*Ancha ...-n*
cold	*chee·*ree	*chiri*
dark	*too·*tah	*tuta*
noisy	*rokh·*yah	*ruqya*

This ... is	*mah·*nahn kai *...·*kah	*Manan kay ...-qa*
not clean.	pee·chas·*kah·*choo	*pichasqachu.*
bed	poo·*nyoo·*nah	*puñuna*
blanket	*kah·*tah/free·*sah·*rah/	*qata/frisara/*
	*choo·*see	*chusi*
house	*wah·*see	*wasi*
pillow	*sow·*nah	*sawna*
room	*kwahr·*too	*kwartu*
towel	ch'ah·kee·chee·*koo·*nah/	*ch'akichikuna/*
	too·*wah·*lyah	*tuwalla*

ACCOMMODATION

HOMESTAYS   QURPACHAKUYKUNA

Homestays are common in smaller communities. In some cases, you may be able to arrange one through a travel agent in the city, but if you're the adventurous sort, you can always trust your luck and try to find one yourself.

Where can I find a place to stay tonight?

mai·*pee·*tahkh   *¿Maypitaq*
poo·nyoo·pah·koo·*rui·*mahn?   *puñupakurquyman?*

Could I/we please spend the night in your house?

ah·*lyee·*choo poo·nyoo·pah·yoo·   *¿Allichu puñupayu-*
kui·kee·*mahn·*choo?;   *kuykimanchu?;*
ah·*lyee·*choo poo·nyoo·pah·yoo·   *¿Allichu puñupayu-*
kui·kee·koo·*mahn·*choo?   *kuykikumanchu?*

We have our own mattresses/ sleeping bags.

poo·nyui·*nai·*koo *kahn·*mee   *Puñunayku kanmi.*

ACCOMMODATION

How much do you charge for ...?	hai·k'ahn kwees·tahn ...?	¿Hayk'an kwistan ...?
each night	sah·pah too·tah	sapa tuta
each day	sah·pah p'oon·chai	sapa p'unchay
both of us	ees·kai·nee·koo·pahkh	iskayni-ykupaq

Thank you, I'd like to stay in your house.

sool·pai·kee, wah·see·kee·pee
kor·pah·chai·tahn
moo·nai·mahn

Sulpayki, wasiykipi
qurpachaytan
munayman.

THEY MAY SAY ...

ah·lyeen·mee, pah·sai·kah·mui
tai·tai/mah·mai
   That's OK. Come in sir/madam.

pahm·pah·chah·yoo·wai mah·nahn
poo·nyoo·nai·koo kahn·choo
   I'm sorry, but we don't have the room.

pahm·pah·chah·yoo·wai mah·nah
roo·nah·koo·nah·tah
qor·pah·chah·chee·koo·choo
   I'm sorry, but we don't take guests.

mai·ken·nee·kee·koo·nahn
qor·pah·chah·koon·kee·chees kai·pee?
   How many of you would like to stay?

hai·k'ah too·tahn poo·nyoo·pah·koon·kee·chees?
   How many nights?

ACCOMMODATION

ACCOMMODATION

DEPARTURE   LLUQSIY

I'm/We're leaving now.
koo·*nahn*·kah   *Kunanqa*
ree·poo·koo·*sahkh*·nyah/   *ripukusaqña/*
ree·poo·koo·sahkh·*koo*·nyah   *ripukusaqkuña.*

Thank you for all your help.
sool·*pai* yah·nah·pah·wahs·   *Sulpáy yanapawa-*
kai·kee·*mahn*·tah   *sqaykimanta.*

Thank you for letting me stay
in your house.
sool·*pai* wah·see·*kee*·pee   *Sulpáy wasiykipi*
kor·pah·chah·chee·wahs·   *qurpachachiwas*
kai·kee·*mahn*·tah/   *qaykimanta/*
poo·nyoo·chee·wahs·   *puñuchiwa-*
kai·kee·*mahn*·tah   *sqaykimanta.*

I hope I can return someday.
ee·*chah*·pahs hai·*k'ahkh*·pahs   *Ichapas hayk'aqpas*
koo·tee·*mui*·mahn   *kutimuyman.*

It was great staying at your place.
seen·*chee*·tah koo·see·*koo*·nee   *Sinchita kusikuni*
wah·see·*kee*·pee   *wasiykipi*
kor·pah·chah·chee·wahs·   *qurpachachiwa-*
kai·kee·*mahn*·tah   *sqaykimanta.*

How much do I owe you?
hai·*k'ah*·tahkh mah·noo·*kui*·kee?   *¿Hayk'ataq manukuyki?*

Here's payment for my stay.
kai kol·*ke*·tah koi·koo·*sai*·kee   *Kay qulqita quykusayki*
wah·see·*kee*·pee   *wasiykipi*
kor·pah·chah·chee·wahs·   *qurpachachiwas*
kai·kee·*mahn*·tah   *qaykimanta.*

LLAQTAPI PURIY
AROUND TOWN

In some villages, Quechua will come in handy at archaeological tourist sites and in shops with Quechua names. Many of the typical nightlife activities and other forms of cosmopolitan entertainment in the larger Andean cities will be organised in Spanish or even in English. Signs will be in Spanish rather than Quechua.

LOOKING FOR ...   ... MASKHAY

Where's a/the ...?	mah·*pee*·tahkh ... kahn?	¿Mapitaq ... kan?
bank	*kol*·keh wah·see	qulqi wasi
hotel	*kor*·pah wah·see	qurpa wasi
main square	*plah*·sah	plasa
market	*k-hah*·too	qhatu
police station	wahr·*dee*·yah	wardiya
post office	koo·*ree*·yoo	kuriyu
public toilet	hees·*p'ah*·koo·nah/ *bah*·nyoo	hisp'akuna/ bañu
telephone centre	tee·lee·foo·*noo*·yokh *wah*·see	tiliphunuyuq wasi
local authorities' office (similar to a town hall)	kah·mah·chekh· *koo*·nahkh *wah*·seen	kamachiq-kunaq wasin

TELECOMMUNICATIONS

IMAYMANA WILLACHIKUYKUNA

Is there a/an ...	*kahn*·choo ...	*¿Kanchu* ...
in this village?	kai lyahkh·*tah*·pee?	*kay llaqtapi?*
computer	koom·poo·tah·*roo*·rah	*kumputarura*
Internet service	een·*teer*·neet	*Intirnit*
telephone	tee·lee·*foo*·noo	*tiliphunu*

It's urgent!
oos·k·hai·*pahkh*·mee!;   *¡Usqhaypaqmi!;*
pree·see·sahkh·*pahkh*·mee!   *¡Prisisaqpaqmi!*

Making a Call

Tiliphunuwan Rimay

Hello.
     nah·pai·koo·*lyai*·kee.   *Napaykullayki.*
This is ... speaking.
     ...n/·mee *kah*·nee   *...-n/-mi kani.*
I'd like to speak to ...
     ...*wahn*·mee ree·*mai*·tah   *...-wanmi rimayta*
     moo·*nah*·nee   *munani.*
Who's calling?
     pee·tahkh *kahm*·kee?   *¿Pitaq kanki?*
Please tell ... I called.
     ah·*lyee*·choo ...·mahn   *Allichu ...-man*
     wee·lyah·poo·*wahn*·kee   *willapuwanki*
     tee·lee·foo·*noo*·pee   *tiliphunupi*
     wahkh·yah·moos·*kai*·tah   *waqyamusqayta.*

AROUND TOWN

SIGHTSEEING

TURISTAKUNA PURISQAN

Where's the tourist office?
mai·*pee*·tahkh
too·rees·tah·koo·*nah*·pahkh
oo·fee·*see*·nah *kah*·shahn?

¿Maypitaq
turistakunapaq
ufisina kashan?

What are the opening hours?
ee·mah oo·*rahs*·mee
kee·chah·*koon*·pees
wees·k'ah·*koon*·pees?

¿Ima urasmi
kichakunpis
wisq'akunpis?

How much is the entry fee?
hai·k'ahn *kwees*·tahn
yai·koo·*nah*·pahkh?

¿Hayk'an kwistan
yaykunapaq?

I'd like to see (Machu Picchu).
(mah·choo *peek*·choo)·tah
k·hah·*wai*·tah/rekh·*see*·tah
moo·*nai*·mahn

(Machu Pikchu)-ta
qhawayta/riqsiyta
munayman.

Can we take photographs here?
foo·too·koo·*nah*·tah
kor·koi·koo·*mahn*·choo
kai·pee?

¿Phutukunata
qurquykumanchu
kaypi?

Could we take photographs of you?
ah·*lyee*·choo foo·*too*·tah
kor·kor·koi·kee·*mahn*·choo?

¿Allichu phututa
qurqurquykimanchu?

Could you take a photograph of me?
ah·*lyee*·choo foo·*too*·tah
kor·kor·ko·wahn·
kee·*mahn*·choo?

¿Allichu phututa
qurqurquwan-
kimanchu?

I'll send you the photographs.
foo·too·koo·*nah*·tah
ah·pah·chee·moo·*sai*·kee

Phutukunata
apachimusayki.

It's ...	...n/·mee	...-n/-mi.
beautiful	*soo*·mahkh	sumaq
impressive	*koo*·sah *koo*·sah	kusa kusa
interesting	*seen*·chee ah·lyeen	sinchi allin
strange	hokh *rek*·ch'ahkh	huq rikch'aq

AROUND TOWN

The Sights   Sumaq K'itikuna

What's that (building)?
> ee·*mah*·tahkh chai   ¿Imataq chay
> (*hah*·toon wah·*se*·kah)?   (hatun wasiqa)?

How old is that (building)?
> hai·k'ah wah·tah·*yokh*·mee   ¿Hayk'a watayuqmi
> chai (*hah*·toon wah·*se*·kah)?   chay hatun wasiqa?

aqueduct	*yahr*·k·hah	yarqha
archaeological site	t·hoo·*nees*·kahkh *nyow*·pah wah·see·*koo*·nah	thunisqa ñawpa wasikuna
burial site	*chooly*·pah	chullpa
cathedral	*hah*·toon een·*lee*·sah	hatun inlisa
church	een·*lee*·sah	inlisa
cave	*mah*·ch'ai	mach'ay
cemetery	*ah*·yah pahm·*pah*·nah	aya pampana
central plaza	*hah*·toon *plah*·sah	hatun plasa
ceremonial baths	*een*·kahkh ahr·mah·*koo*·nahn	Inkaq armakunan
crowded	*ahs*·k·hah roo·nah·*koo*·nah	askha runakuna
dance	*too*·sui	tusuy
doorway	hai·*koo*·nah *poon*·koo	haykuna punku
festival	*rai*·mee	raymi
fortress	poo·*kah*·rah	pukara
gate	*hah*·toon *poon*·koo	hatun punku
Inca trail	*een*·kah poo·*rees*·kahn nyahn	Inka purisqan ñan
monastery	*ahk*·lyah *wah*·see; moo·nahs·tee·*ree*·yoo	aklla wasi; munastiriyu
museum	moo·*see*·yoo	musiyu
niche	*oos*·noo/*t'o*·ko	usnu/t'uqu
offering	hai·wah·*ree*·kui	haywarikuy
park	pook·*lyah*·nah *pahm*·pah; *pahr*·kee	pukllana pampa; parki

principal temple	*hah·*toon *mahn·*kos *wah·*see	*hatun manqus wasi*
royal palace	*kees·*wahr/*hah·*toon *kahn·*chah	*kiswar/hatun kancha*
royal tomb	*chooly·*pah	*chullpa*
ruins	*rah·*kai *rah·*kai; t-hoo·*nees·*kah wah·see·*koo·*nah	*raqay raqay; thunisqa wasikuna*
settlement	*lyahkh·*tah/*ai·*lyoo	*llaqta/ayllu*
statue	*reek·*ch'ai/ ees·tah·*too·*wah	*rikch'ay/ istatuwa*
temple	*mahn·*kos *wah·*see	*manqus wasi*
temple of the Sun	ko·ree·*kahn·*chah	*Qurikancha*
textile/weaving	*ah·*wah	*awa*
volcano	*nee·*nah p-*hokh·*chekh *or·*ko	*nina phuqchiq urqu*
warrior	*ow·*kah *poo·*rekh	*awqa puriq*
window	k-hah·wah·*ree·*nah/*t'o·*ko	*qhawarina/t'uqu*

AROUND TOWN

Tours

Turistakuna Purinan

How much is a guide?
> hai·*k'ah*·tahkh *koob*·rahn
> poo·sai·*kah*·chahkh *roo*·nah?

¿Hayk'ataq kubran pusaykachaq runa?

Could we hire an English-speaking/ Spanish-speaking guide?
> meen·*k'ah*·kui·koo·*mahn*·choo
> *een*·lees/kahs·tee·*lyah*·noo
> *ree*·mahkh poo·sai·kah·*chahkh*·tah?

¿Mink'akuykumanchu inlis/kastillanu rimaq pusaykachaqta?

I'm with them.
> pai·koo·nah·*wahn*·mee
> kah·*shah*·nee

Paykunawanmi kashani.

I've lost my group.
> too·rees·tah·mah·see·koo·*nah*·tahn
> cheen·kah·chee·koor·*ko*·nee

Turistamasikunatan chinkachikurquni.

Have you seen a group of foreigners?
> k·hah·wahr·*kahn*·*kee*·choo
> *hah*·wah roo·nah·koo·*nah*·tah?

¿Qhawarqankichu hawa runakunata?

YOU SAY POTATO ...

Historically, there have been more than 80 distinct ways of writing the name of the Quechua language. This was due mostly to variations in regional pronunciations, and also to a misanalysis of the relationship between different sounds. Some examples: *cjeswa*, *kechwa*, *khetsua*, *kichwa*, *kkechuwa*, *keshua*, *keswa*, *qheswa*, *q'eswa*, *qhexwa*, *quichua* and *qqichua*. In modern times, with the increasing standardisation of the Quechua alphabet, some researchers have proposed the following spellings: *kichwa*, *qhiswa* and *qichwa*.

GOING OUT

MAYTAPAS RIY

'Going out' in smaller communities is generally limited to visiting neighbours or attending local festivities.

This place is great.
kai lyahkh·*tah*·kah/fees·*tah*·kah
seen·chee soo·*mahkh*·mee

Kay llaqtaqa/phistaqa sinchi sumaqmi.

I'm having a good time here.
k'o·choo·ree·koo·*shah*·neen
kai·pee

Q'uchurikushanin kaypi.

Shall we go somewhere else?
pahkh·tah mai·*tah*·pahs
reen·*chees*·mahn?

¿Paqta maytapas rinchisman?

I'm sorry, I'm a terrible dancer.
dees·peen·sah·*yoo*·wai, *mah*·nahn
koo·*sah*·tah too·soo·*nee*·choo

Dispinsayuway, manan kusata tusunichu.

Where to Go

Maytan Rinkiman

What's there to do in the evenings?
ee·mah·*tah*·tahkh roo·nah·*koo*·nah
too·*tah*·pee roo·*wahn*·koo
k'o·choo·ree·koo·nahn·*koo*·pahkh?

¿Imatataq runakuna tutapi ruwanku q'uchurikunankupaq?

What shall we do tonight?
ee·mah·*tah*·tahkh
roo·wahn·*chees*·mahn
koo·nahn too·*tah*?

¿Imatataq ruwanchisman kunan tuta?

Are there musicians?
kahn·choo moo·see·koo·*koo*·nah?

¿Kanchu musikukuna?

AROUND TOWN

I feel like going to a/the ...	...·man *ree*·tah moo·*nai*·mahn	...-man riyta munayman.
chicha bar	*ah*·k-hah *wah*·see	aqha wasi
local fiesta	kai lyahkh·*tah*·pee *fees*·tah	kay llaqtapi phista
restaurant	mee·*k-hoo*·nah *wah*·see	mikhuna wasi

I'd like to ...	...tah moo·*nai*·mahn	...-ta munayman.
dance	*too*·sui	tusuy
drink coffee/	*kah*·feel/	kaphiy/
tea	*tee*·tah *ook*·yai	tiyta ukyay
walk	*poo*·ree	puriy

Invitations   Inwitasiyunkuna

What are you doing this evening?
ee·mah·*tah*·tahkh *koo*·nahn *too*·tah roo·*wahn*·kee?
¿Imatataq kunan tuta ruwanki?

Would you like to go out somewhere today/tomorrow?
mai·*tah*·pahs *ree*·tah moo·nahn·kee·*mahn*·choo *koo*·nahn/pah·*kah*·reen?
¿Maytapas riyta munankimanchu kunan/paqarin?

Would you like to go for a drink?
ee·mah·lyah·*tah*·pees *ook*·yah·*nah*·pahkh mai·*tah*·pees *ree*·tah moo·nahn·kee·*mahn*·choo?
¿Imallatapis ukyanapaq maytapis riyta munankimanchu?

Would you like to go for a meal?
ee·mah·lyah·*tah*·pees mee·k-hoo·*nah*·pahkh mai·*tah*·pees *ree*·tah moo·nahn·kee·*mahn*·choo?
¿Imallatapis mikhunapaq maytapis riyta munankimanchu?

Do you know a good restaurant?
rekh·seen·*kee*·choo hokh *soo*·makh mee·*k-hoo*·nah wah·*see*·tah?
¿Riqsinkichu huq sumaq mikhuna wasita?

My shout/treat. (I'll buy)
no·kahn een·wee·tah·*sai*·kee   *Nuqan inwitasayki.*
Do you want to go to the ...?
...·tah *ree*·tah   *¿...-ta riyta*
moo·nahn·*kee*·choo?   *munankichu?*
Come on!/Let's go!
hah·koo!/hah·*koo*·chee!   *¡Haku!/¡Hakuchi!*

Responding to Invitations
Inwitasiyunkunata Kutichiy

Sure!
ah·*lyeen*·mee!   *¡Allinmi!*
Yes, I'd love to.
ah·*ree*, moo·nai·*mahn*·mee   *Arí, munaymanmi.*
Yes. Where shall we go?
ah·*ree*. mai·*tah*·tahkh   *Arí. ¿Maytataq*
reen·*chees*·mahn?   *rinchisman?*
No. I'm afraid I can't.
mah·nahn *ree*·tah   *Manan riyta*
ah·tee·*nee*·choo   *atinichu.*
I don't have time.
mah·nahn *teem*·pui *kahn*·choo   *Manan timpuy kanchu.*
What about tomorrow?
ee·mah·*tah*·tahkh roo·*wahm*·kee   *¿Imatataq ruwanki*
pah·*kah*·reen?   *paqarin?*

Arranging to Meet
Tinkunapaq Rimanakuy

What time shall we meet?
ee·mah oo·*rahs*·mee   *¿Ima urasmi*
teen·koo·*soon*·chees?   *tinkusunchis?*
Where shall we meet?
mai·peen teen·koo·*soon*·chees?   *¿Maypin tinkusunchis?*
Let's meet (at eight o'clock) at the ...
(lahs *oo*·choo oo·*rahs*·tah)   *(Las uchu urasta)*
teen·*koo*·soon ...·pee   *Tinkusun ...-pi.*

AROUND TOWN

OK. I'll see you then.
koo·sah   Kusa.
too·pahn·ahn·chees·kah·mah   Tupananchiskama.
Agreed!/OK!
ah·lyeen·mee!/koo·sah!   ¡Allinmi!/¡Kusa!
I'll come over at (six/eight) o'clock.
(lahs sah·yees/lahs oo·choo)   (Las sayis/Las uchu)
oo·rahs·tah hah·moo·sahkh.   Urasta hamusaq.
I'll try to make it.
ah·tees·pah mah·nah   Atispa mana
ah·tees·pah·pees   atispapis
hah·moo·sahkh·mee   hamusaqmi.
I'll be along later.
ahs·wahn k·he·pah·tah·rahkh·mee Aswan qhipataraqmi
hah·moo·sahkh.   hamusaq.
Where will you be?
mai·peen kahn·kee?   ¿Maypin kanki?
See you later/tomorrow.
too·pah·nahn·chees·kah·mah/   Tupananchiskama/
pah·kah·reen·kah·mah   Paqarinkama.
Sorry I'm late.
pahm·pah·chah·yoo·wai   Pampachayuway
k·he·pah·ree·koos·khai·mahn·tah qhiparikusqaymanta.

FAMILY

The family is the highest priority for every individual in Andean society. Extended families are the norm, with parents, children, grandparents and sometimes other relatives living together. Kinship often extends beyond the biological family through marriage and a system where godparents are expected to act as a second set of parents to a child. The more children you have, the more godparents, and thus the larger the extended family and community, known as an *ayllu*, *ai*·lyoo.

Romantic relationships, marital status and children are common topics of conversation for young people.

QUESTIONS & ANSWERS

TAPUYKUNAPIS KUTICHIYKUNAPIS

Are you married? (asked to a woman)
  ko·sah·*yokh*·choo/
  kah·sah·*roo*·choo *kahn*·kee?   *¿Qusayuqchu/ Kasaruchu kanki?*

Are you married? (asked to a man)
  wahr·mee·*yokh*·choo/
  kah·sah·*roo*·choo *kahn*·kee?   *¿Warmiyuqchu/ Kasaruchu kanki?*

I'm (a) ...	*no*·kah ...·n/·mee *kah*·nee	*Nuqa* ...·n/·mi *kani.*
divorced	t'ah·qah·nah·*koos*·kah/ t'ah·*kahs*·kah	*t'aqanakusqa/ t'aqasqa*
married (f)	ko·*sah*·yokh	*qusayuq*
married (m)	wahr·*mee*·yokh	*warmiyuq*
separated	t'ah·*kahs*·kah	*t'aqasqa*
single (f)	sool·*tee*·rah; mah·nah ko·*sah*·yokh	*sultira; mana qusayuq*
single (m)	sool·*tee*·roo; mah·nah wahr·*mee*·yokh	*sultiru; mana warmiyuq*
widow	*wahr*·mee *sah*·pah	*warmi sapa*
widower	*sah*·pahn k·*hah*·ree	*sapan qhari*

FAMILY

I have a partner.

yah·nah·*yokh*·mee *kah*·nee	*Yanayuqmi kani.*

We live together
but we're not married.

no·*kai*·koo koos·*kai*·koon	*Nuqayku kuskaykun*
tee·*yai*·koo,	*tiyayku,*
ee·*chah*·kah *mah*·nahn	*ichaqa manan*
kah·sah·rah·koos·*kah*·choo kai·koo	*kasarakusqachu kayku.*

The word 'child' isn't used by men, who must always specify the
sex of their children. Women, however, can be asked or might
say these phrases:

How many ... do you have?	*hai*·k'ahn ...?	*¿Hayk'an ...?*
children	wah·wai·kee·*koo*·nah	*wawaykikuna*
sons	k·*hah*·ree	*qhari*
	wah·wai·kee·*koo*·nah	*wawaykikuna*
daughters	*wahr*·mee	*warmi*
	wah·wai·kee·*koo*·nah	*wawaykikuna*

I don't have any children.

mah·nahn wah·wai·*koo*·nai	*Manan wawaykunay.*

I have ... daughter(s)/son(s).

...·n/·mee *wahr*·mee/·k-*hah*·ree	*...·n/·mi warmi/qhari*
wah·wai(*koo*·nah)	*waway(kuna).*

How many brothers/sisters
do you have?

hai·k'ahn too·rai·kee·*koo*·nah/	*¿Hayk'an turaykikuna/*
nyah·nyai·kee·*koo*·nah?	*ñañaykikuna?*

Men can be asked or might say these phrases:

How many ... do you have?	*hai*·k'ahn ...?	*¿Hayk'an ...?*
sons	choo·ree·*koo*·nah	*churiykuna*
daughters	oo·soo·see·kee·*koo*·nah	*ususiykikuna*

I don't have any sons/daughters.
mah·nahn choo·ree·*koo*·nah/   *Manan churiykuna/*
oo·soo·see·*koo*·nah kahn·choo   *ususiykuna kanchu.*

I have ... daughter(s)/son(s).
...n/·mee *choo*·ree(*koo*·nah)/   *...-n/·mi churiy(kuna)/*
oo·soo·see(*koo*·nah)   *ususiy(kuna).*

How many brothers/sisters
do you have?
hai·k'ahn wow·kay·kee·*koo*·nah/   *¿Hayk'an wawqiykikuna/*
pah·nai·kee·*koo*·nah?   *panaykikuna?*

Both men and women can be asked or might say:

How old are they?
hai·k'ah wah·tah·*yokh*·mee   *¿Hayk'a watayuqmi*
pai·*koo*·nah kahn·koo?   *paykuna kanku?*

Do you live with your family?
ai·lyui·kee·*wahn*·choo/   *¿Aylluykiwanchu/*
fah·mee·lyai·kee·*wahn*·choo   *phamillaykiwanchu*
tee·*yahm*·kee?   *tiyanki?*

I live with my family.
ai·lyui·*wahn*·mee tee·*yah*·nee   *Aylluywanmi tiyani.*

Do you have a girlfriend/boyfriend?
yah·nah·*yokh*·choo *kahn*·kee?   *¿Yanayuqchu kanki?*

THE PERFECT ENDING

Remember, when using the *-n/-mi* suffix, choose
the *-n* ending when the preceding root word ends
in a vowel, and the *-mi* ending when it ends in
a consonant. Note that using the *-mi* ending
will change which syllable is stressed. This is a
general rule in this book.

FAMILY

FAMILY MEMBERS   AYLLUKUNA

aunt	*tee*·yah	*tiya*
baby	*wah*·wah/	*wawa/*
	wah·*wah*·chah	*wawacha*
boy	*er*·ke/*makh*·tah	*irqi/maqta*
boyfriend	*yah*·nah	*yana*
brother (of a woman)	*too*·rah/*too*·ree	*tura/turi*
brother (of a man)	*wai*·ke/*wow*·ke	*wayqi/wawqi*
child (of a woman)	*wah*·wah	*wawa*
daughter (of a woman)	*wahr*·mee *wah*·wah	*warmi wawa*
daughter (of a man)	oo·*soo*·see;	*ususi;*
	wahr·mee *choo*·ree	*warmi churi*
family	*ai*·lyoo/	*ayllu/*
	fah·*mee*·lyah	*phamilla*
father	*tai*·tah/*pah*·pah/	*tayta/papa/*
	tah·tah	*tata*
father-in-law	*sui*·roo	*suyru*
girl	*p'ahs*·nyah/*see*·pahs/	*p'asña/sipas/*
	see·*pahs*·chah	*sipascha*
girlfriend	*yah*·nah	*yana*
grandchild	*hah*·wai	*haway*
grandfather	*hah*·toon *tai*·tah	*hatun tayta*
	ah·*poo*·chah;	*apucha;*
	mah·*choo*·lah;	*machula;*
	hah·*too*·koo;	*hatuku;*
	ah·*wee*·loo	*awilu*
grandmother	*hah*·toon *mah*·mah;	*hatun mama;*
	ah·*wee*·lah	*awila*
husband	*ko*·sah	*qusa*
mother	*mah*·mah	*mama*
mother-in-law	*sui*·rah	*suyra*
parents	*tai*·tah·*mah*·mah	*taytamama*
sister (of a woman)	*nyah*·nyah	*ñaña*
sister (of a man)	*pah*·nah/*pah*·nee	*pana/pani*
son (of a woman)	k·*hah*·ree *wah*·wah	*qhari wawa*

son (of a man)	*choo·ree*	*churi*
stepfather	*k-he·pah tai·tah*	*qhipa tayta*
stepmother	*k-he·pah mah·mah*	*qhipa mama*
uncle	*tee·yoo*	*tiyu*
wife	*wahr·mee*	*warmi*

TALKING WITH PARENTS	**TAYTAMAMAKUNAWAN RIMAY**

When's the baby due?
    hai·*k'ahkh*·mee wah·chah·*koon*·kee?

        ¿Hayk'aqmi wachakunki?

What are you going to call your baby?
    ee·*mah*·tahkh wah·*wai*·kekh *soo*·teen *kahn*·kah?

        ¿Imataq wawaykiq sutin kanqa?

Women can be asked or might say these phrases:

Is this your first child?
    p-*hee*·wee wah·*wai*·kee·choo pai?

        ¿Phiwi wawaykichu pay?

How old are your children?
    hai·*k'ah* wah·tah·*yohkh*·mee wah·*wai*·kee·*koo*·nah?

        ¿Hayk'a watayuqmi wawaykikuna?

Men can be asked or might say:

How old are your sons/daughters?
    hai·*k'ah* wah·tah·*yohkh*·mee choo·*ree*·kee·*koo*·nah/ oo·*soo*·see·kee·*koo*·nah?

        ¿Hayk'a watayuqmi churiykikuna/ ususiykikuna?

FAMILY

FAMILY FAVOURS

Mutual cooperation among families and members of the *ayllu, ai·*lyoo, 'extended family', is a way of life. *Ayni, ai·*nee, 'reciprocal labour', assures that if you do someone a favour or lend them something today, they'll return the favour tomorrow. A similar concept is *mink'a, meen·*k'ah, which means 'cooperation' or 'collaboration'.

Incredible! You look so young!
*mah·*nah ee·*nyee·*nah!	*¡Mana iñina!*
*see·*pahs/*wai·*nah	*Sipas/Wayna*
*hee·*nah kah·*shahn·*kee	*hina kashanki.*

Does she/he attend school?
*yah·*chai wah·*see·*tah reen·choo?	*¿Yachay wasita rinchu?*

Who looks after the children?
*pee·*tahkh	*¿Pitaq*
wahr·mah·chah·koo·*nah·*tah	*warmachakunata*
k·*hah·*wahn?	*qhawan?*

Do you have grandchildren?
hah·wai·kee·*koo·*nah *kahn·*choo?	*¿Hawaykikuna kanchu?*

What's your baby's name?
ee·*mah·*tahkh wah·wah·*chai·*kekh	*¿Imataq wawachaykiq*
*soo·*teen?	*sutin?*

Is it a boy or a girl?
er·*ke·*choo ee·chah	*¿Irqichu icha*
p'ahs·*nyah·*choo?	*p'asñachu?*

Does she/he let you sleep at night?
poo·*nyoon·*choo too·*tah·*pee?	*¿Puñunchu tutapi?*

What a beautiful child!
ee·mah *soo·*makh *wah·*wah!	*¡Ima sumaq wawa!*

She/He looks like you.
*pai·*kah kahn·*mahn·*mee	*Payqa qanmanmi*
reekh·*ch'ah·*koon	*rikch'akun.*

FAMILY

TALKING WITH CHILDREN

WARMAKUNAWAN RIMAY

What's your name?
ee·mahn soo·*tee*·kee?

¿Iman sutiyki?

How old are you?
hai·k'ah wah·tah·chah·*yokh*·mee
kahn·kee?

¿Hayk'a watachayuqmi
kanki?

When's your birthday?
hai·*k'ahkh*·mee
wah·t'a hoon·t'ai·*nee*·kee?

¿Hayk'aqmi
wat'a hunt'ayniki?

Do you have brothers and sisters?
(said to a girl)
too·rah·nyah·nyah·*yokh*·choo
kahn·kee?

¿Tura-ñañayuqchu
kanki?

Do you have brothers and sisters?
(said to a boy)
wow·ke·pah·nah·*yokh*·choo
kahn·kee?

¿Wawqi-panayuqchu
kanki?

Do you go to school?
yah·chai wah·*see*·tah/
ees·kui·*lah*·tah reen·*kee*·choo?

¿Yachay wasita/
iskuylata rinkichu?

Do you like school?
moo·nahn·*kee*·choo *yah*·chai
wah·*see*·tah/ees·kui·*lah*·tah?

¿Munankichu yachay
wasita/iskuylata?

Is your teacher nice?
ah·lyeen roo·*nah*·choo
yah·chah·chekh·*nee*·kee?

¿Allin runachu
yachachiqniyki?

Do you play soccer?
pee·*loo*·tah hai·*t'ai*·tah
pookh·lyahn·*kee*·choo?

¿Piluta hayt'ayta
pukllankichu?

What kind of games do you play?
ee·mah
pookh·lyai·koo·*nah*·tahn
pookh·*lyahn*·kee?

¿Ima
pukllaykunatan
pukllanki?

Do you study English?
een·lees see·*mee*·tah
yah·chahn·*kee*·choo?

¿Inlis simita
yachankichu?

Do you want to play?
 pookh·*lyai*·tah
 moo·nahn·*kee*·choo?

¿Pukllayta
munankichu?

What shall we play?
 ee·mah·*tah*·tahkh
 pookh·lyahn·*chees*·mahn?

¿Imatataq
pukllanchisman?

Do you have a pet at home?
 chee·*tai*·kee *kahn*·choo
 wah·see·*kee*·pee?

¿Chitayki kanchu
wasiykipi?

MUNASQANCHISKUNAPAS RUWANANCHISKUNAPAS
INTERESTS & ACTIVITIES

Some activities that Westerners think of as hobbies, such as gardening, walking and cooking, are still very much a way of life for Andean people.

COMMON INTERESTS		KAQLLA MUNASQANCHISKUNA
What do you do in your spare time?		
ee·mah·*tah*·tahkh roo·*wahn*·kee teem·*pui*·kee *kahkh*·teen?		¿Imatataq ruwanki timpuyki kaqtin?
Do you like ...?	...tah moo·nahn·*kee*·choo?	¿...-ta munankichu?
I like ...	...tah moo·*nah*·neen	...-ta munanin.
I don't like ...	*mah*·nahn ...tah moo·nah·*nee*·choo	Manan ...-ta munanichu.
cooking	*wai*·k'ui	wayk'uy
dancing	*too*·sui	tusuy
fishing	*chahly*·wai; *chahly*·*wah*·kui; *chahly*·wah *hah*·p'ee	challway; challwakuy; challwa hap'iy
food	mee·*k*·*hoo*·nah	mikhuna
getting together with friends	k·*hoo*·yah·nah·kokh· mah·see·koo·*nah*·wahn hoo·nyoo·*nah*·kui	khuyanakuq- masikunawan huñunakuy
hiking	*poo*·ree	puriy
hunting	*hah*·p'ee/*chah*·kui	hap'iy/chakuy
music	moo·*see*·kah	musika
reading	*lee*·yee/ nyah·*ween*·chai	liyiy/ ñawinchay
singing	*tah*·kee	takiy
talking	*ree*·mai	rimay

INTERESTS & ACTIVITIES

I make ...	...·tahn roo·*wah*·nee	...-tan ruwani
clothes	p'ah·chah·*koo*·nah	*p'achakuna*
embroidery	*wel*·k'oy	*wilq'uy*
handicrafts	ahr·tee·sah·*nee*·yah	*artisaniya*
jewellery	*ee*·lyah/oo·*mee*·nyah	*illa/umiña*
pottery	*rakh*·ch'ee/*k'akh*·rah	*raqch'i/k'akra*
textiles	ah·wai·*koo*·nah	*awaykuna*

carve (only stone)	*koo*·chui/*ch'e*·koi	*kuchuy/ch'iquy*
draw	se·*ken*·chai	*siq'inchay*
embroider	*wel*·k'oy	*wilq'uy*
paint	*lyoo*·see/*peen*·tai	*llusiy/pintay*
sew	*see*·rai	*siray*
spin (thread or yarn)	*pooch*·kai/*poos*·kai	*puchkay/puskay*
weave	*ah*·wai	*away*

SPORT   PUKLLAYKUNA

What sport do you play?
  ee·mah pookh·lyai·koo·*nah*·tahn pookh·*lyan*·kee?   *¿Ima pukllaykunatan pukllanki?*

I play soccer/volleyball.
  [pee·*loo*·tah hai·*t'ai*·tah; boo·*lee*·tah] pookh·*lyah*·nee   *[piluta hayt'ay-ta; bulita] pukllani.*

I can swim.
  wai·*t'ai*·tah yah·*chah*·nee   *Wayt'ayta yachani.*

I like to run.
  pah·*wai*·tahn moo·*nah*·nee   *Pawaytan munani.*

I like fishing.
  chahly·wah hah·*p'ee*·tahn moo·*nah*·nee   *Challwa hap'itan munani.*

I know how to bullfight.
  too·roo pookh·*lyai*·tah yah·*chah*·nee   *Turu pukllayta yachani.*

INTERESTS &
ACTIVITIES

Do you like sports?
pook·lyai·koo·*nah*·tah   *¿Pukllaykunata*
moo·nahn·*kee*·choo?   *munankichu?*
Yes, very much.
ah·*ree*, ahn·*chah*·tahn   *Arí, anchatan*
moo·*nah*·nee   *munani.*
No, not at all.
mah·nahn moo·nah·*nee*·choo   *Manan munanichu.*
I like watching sport.
k-hah·wai·*lyah*·tah moo·*nah*·nee   *Qhawayllata munani.*

Talking about   ## Piluta Hayt'aymanta
Soccer   ## Rimay

Do you follow soccer?
pee·*loo*·tah hai·*t'ai*·tah   *¿Piluta hayt'ayta*
pah·sahkh koo·*tee*·lyah   *pasaq kutilla*
k-hah·wahn·*kee*·choo?   *qhawankichu?*
Which team do you support?
mai·ken·*neen*·tahkh   *¿Mayqinnintaq*
ee·kee·*pui*·kee?   *ikipuyki?*
Who's winning?
mai·ken·*neen*·tahkh   *¿Mayqinnintaq*
lyah·*lyee*·shahn?   *llallishan?*
Do you play in a team?
ee·kee·*poo*·pee   *¿Ikipupi*
pookh·lyahn·*kee*·choo?   *pukllankichu?*
Do you want to play soccer?
pee·*loo*·tah hai·*t'ai*·tah   *¿Piluta hayt'ayta*
moo·nahn·*kee*·choo?   *munankichu?*

THEY MAY YELL ...

gool!	Goal!
pee·nahl!	Penalty!
ow·sai!	Offside!
tee·roo *lyoo*·ree!	Free kick!

INTERESTS & ACTIVITIES

MUSIC   *MUSIKA*

Traditional Andean music takes a variety of forms. The best known include the *waynu*, *wai·noo*, which can be fast or slow, happy or sad; the *harawi*, hah·*rah*·wee, typically a sweet but sad song; the *waylas*, *wai*·lahs, a fast melody; and the *sikuri*, see·*koo*·ree, which starts out slowly but gradually increases in tempo. It's often used to express Andean spiritual tradition and is popular in worship ceremonies. Each style of music is performed using distinctive instruments, and has its own dance variations.

The *cumbia*, *koom*·bya, is popular throughout the Andes, as is the *chicha*, *chee*·chah, genre: a mixture of coastal *cumbia* and the *waynu* (not to be confused with the popular drink *chicha*).

RATTLE AND HUM

Since pre-Columbian times, the instruments of the Andes have included various types of panpipes, flutes, drums, a guitar-like instrument made from an armadillo shell and leg rattles made of pig or goat hooves. In modern times, guitars, violins and harps have been added to the traditional repertoire of instruments, encouraging innovation in the styles and rhythms of Andean music.

Generally, Quechua speakers are very pleased to talk about music and instruments, as they have profound meaning in their lives.

antara/rundadur   ahn·*tah*·rah/roon·*dah*·door
  panpipe of bamboo, with a single row of pipes.
  It's called a *rundadur* in Ecuador only.
chaqchas/chullus   chahkh·chahs/*choo*·lyoos
  Bolivian leg rattle, made of ribbon with goat or pig
  hooves woven onto it

INTERESTS &
ACTIVITIES

RATTLE AND HUM (cont.)

charangu/kirkinchu   chah·*rahn*·goo/
keer·*keen*·choo
   small Andean ten-string guitar, made of armadillo
   shell or carved wood

harpa   *hahr*·pah
   harp

kañari/   kah·*nyah*·ree/
waqraphuku   wahkh·rah·*p*-hoo·koo
   Andean horn, made from a cow's horn

pinkuyllu   peen·*kui*·lyoo
   Andean long flute, made from hardwood

pututu   poo·*too*·too
   conch shell horn

qina   *ke*·nah
   Andean flute, made from bone or hardwood

siku   *see*·koo
   panpipe of cane or bamboo, with two rows of pipes

tinya   *teen*·yah
   tambourine or small drum, made from tree bark and
   goat skin

ukarina   oo·kah·*ree*·nah
   Andean globular flute

wankar   *wahn*·kahr
   mid-sized Andean drum of sheep skin

wankara   wahn·*kah*·rah
   large, round Andean drum, made of wood, shell and
   goat skin

waylachu   wai·*lah*·choo
   devil *charango*; has metal strings that produce a
   sharp sound

wiyulin   wee·*yoo*·leen
   violin or fiddle

INTERESTS & ACTIVITIES

Do you like ...?	...·tah moo·nahn·*kee*·choo?	¿...-ta munankichu?
listening to music	moo·see·*kah*·tah oo·*yah*·ree	musikata uyariy
dancing	*too*·sui	tusuy

Do you know how to play ...?
...·tah wah·kah·cheen·*kee*·choo?   ¿...-ta waqachinkichu?

I play ...
...·tah wah·kah·*chee*·nee   ...-ta waqachini.

Where can I hear traditional music around here?
mai·*pee*·tahkh
see·koo·ree·koo·*nah*·tah
oo·*yah*·reer·*koi*·mahn kai
lyahkh·*tah*·pee?

¿Maypitaq
sikurikunata
uyarirquyman kay
llaqtapi?

INTERESTS &
ACTIVITIES

TALKING ABOUT TRAVELLING

PURIYMANTA RIMAY

I've been travelling for (two) months.
(*ees*·kai) kee·*lyah*·nyahn
poo·*ree*·lyah poo·ree·*koo*·nee

(Iskay) killañan
purilla purikuni.

I'm going to ...
...·*sahkh*·mee

...-saqmi.

I've been to ...
...·pee poo·ree·moor·*kah*·nee

...-pi purimurqani.

Is it safe for women travellers
on their own?
ah·*leen*·choo sah·pah·*lyahn*·koo
wahr·mee·*koo*·nah *chai*·pee
poo·ree·moo·nahn·*koo*·pahkh?

¿Allinchu sapallanku
warmikuna chaypi
purimunankupaq?

I thought it was ...	...·ch/·chah chai *nees*·pah *nee*·nee	...-ch/-cha chay nispa nini.
boring	*mah*·nah *ah*·lyeen	mana allin
great	ee·mah *soo*·mahkh	ima sumaq
horrible	*mee*·lyai	millay
OK	*koo*·sah	kusa
too expensive	*ahn*·chah chah·*nee*·yokh	ancha chaniyuq

STAYING IN TOUCH

ATUNAKUKUY

Tomorrow is my last day here.
pah·kah·reen·kah·*mah*·lyahn
kai·pee *kah*·sahkh

Paqarinkamallan
kaypi kasaq.

Let's swap addresses.
dee·reek·see·yoon·neen·*chees*·tah
koi·koo·nah·koo·soon·*yah*

Diriksiyunninchista
quykunakusunyá.

I'll send you copies of the photos.
foo·too·*koo*·nahkh
koo·pee·*yahn*·tah
ah·pah·chee·moo·*sai*·keen

Phutukunaq
kupiyanta
apachimusaykin.

I'll write to you.
kel·kah·moo·*sai*·keen

Qilqamusaykin.

INTERESTS & ACTIVITIES

It's been great meeting you.

| ahn·*chah*·tahn koo·see·*koo*·nee | *Anchatan kusikuni* |
| rekh·see·koos·*pai*·kee | *riqsikuspayki.* |

Keep in touch!

| kel·kah·nah·koo·soon·*yah!/* | *¡Qilqanakusunyá!/* |
| wah·too·nah·koo·koo·soon·*yah!* | *¡Watunakukusunyá!* |

PUTTING THE RECORD STRAIGHT

The early colonial period (1532–1820s) produced two important literary works by *misti, mees-tee,* mixed-blood authors, still well known today.

The Royal Commentaries of the Incas and General History of Peru (1609), by Garcilaso de la Vega, compares the greatness of the Inca civilization with the great classical civilizations of Western history. The author, the son of an Inca princess and a Spanish conquistador, felt the need to validate his indigenous heritage through comparison with his Spanish roots. While the work is in Spanish, it's main thrust is to glorify the Inca empire, putting it on par with the Roman empire that gave rise to the Spanish empire.

The second work is *New Chronicle and Good Government* (1615), by Felipe Guaman Poma de Ayala. His 1300-page letter to the Spanish king is written in a complex combination of Spanish and Quechua, interspersed with other indigenous languages. He offers anecdotes from indigenous life before the conquest, to illustrate how poorly the King's representatives in the New World were faring in their administrative tasks.

TREKKING

Wilderness adventures and trekking are excellent ways to explore some of the more remote communities and archaeological sites. Companies based in highland cities specialise in arranging treks and mountain climbing expeditions. The local guides and porters often speak Quechua.

GETTING INFORMATION — TAPUKUY

Where can I find out about
hiking trails in the region?
    pee·*tah*·tahkh tah·*pui*·mahn
    kai lyahkh·*tah*·pee poo·*ree*·nah
    nyahn·koo·nah·*mahn*·tah?
    *¿Pitataq tapuyman
    kay llaqtapi purina
    ñankunamanta?*

Who knows the hiking trails?
    pee·tahkh poo·*ree*·nah
    nyahn·koo·*nah*·tah *rekh*·seen?
    *¿Pitaq purina
    ñankunata riqsin?*

Do we need a guide?
    moo·nai·koo·*mahn*·choo
    nyahn rekh·see·*chekh*·tah?
    *¿Munaykumanchu
    ñan riqsichiqta?*

Are there guided treks here?
    kahn·choo nyahn
    rekh·see·chekh·koo·nah *kai*·pee?
    *¿Kanchu ñan
    riqsichiqkuna kaypi?*

Will you guide me?
    poo·sah·wahn·kee·*mahn*·choo?
    ¿Pusawankimanchu?

How long is the trail?
    mai·kah·*mah*·tahkh
    poo·reen·*chees*·mahn?
    *¿Maykamataq
    purinchisman?*

Is the track well-marked?
    ah·lyeen oo·nahn·chahs·*kah*·choo
    chai nyahn?
    *¿Allin unanchasqachu
    chay ñan?*

Which is the shortest route?
    mai·*ken*·tahkh *ahs*·wahn
    pee·see poo·*ree*·nah?
    *¿Mayqintaq aswan
    pisi purina?*

Which is the easiest route?
    mai·*ken*·tahkh *mah*·nah
    sah·sah poo·*ree*·nah?
    *¿Mayqintaq mana
    sasa purina?*

TREKKING

ALTITUDE SICKNESS

Altitude sickness, *suruchi*, soo·roo·chee, is always a real concern when travelling anywhere in the Andes. Symptoms include:

breathlessness	*mana samayniyuq*
	mah·nah sah·mai·nee·yokh
dizziness	*uma muyuy*
	oo·mah moo·yui
fatigue	*sayk'uy*
	sai·k'ui
headache	*uma nanay*
	oo·mah nah·nai
insomnia	*mana puñuy atipay*
	mah·nah poo·nyui ah·tee·pai
mental confusion	*yuyay pantay*
	yoo·yai pahn·tai
nausea	*millanayay*
	mee·lyah·nah·yai
a pounding heart	*sunqu phatatatay*
	son·ko p·hah·tah·tah·tai

If you're on the trail and start to notice symptoms, try to move to a lower altitude immediately. Glucose tablets may also help. Chewing coca leaves, *kuka matu*, koo·kah mah·too, is a local remedy that Andeans have used for centuries. If you can't bring yourself to do that, coca leaf tea, *kuka mati*, koo·kah mah·tee, might also do the trick. If you're in a city and you experience symptoms, rest and get acclimatised – drink plenty of water – before trying any strenuous activities such as trekking, even for short day trips. Seek medical assistance if the symptoms persist.

How many hours will it take?
hai·k'ah oo·*rahs*·peen
chai·mahn chah·*yahn*·chees?

¿Hayk'a uraspin
chayman chayanchis?

Is the path open?
kee·chahs·*kah*·choo
nyahn *kah*·shahn?

¿Kichasqachu
ñan kashan?

Is it safe to climb this mountain?
wee·chah·*nah*·pahkh
ah·*lyeen*·choo kai *or*·ko?

¿Wichanapaq
allinchu kay urqu?

How high is the climb?
mai·kah·*mah*·tahkh
wee·chahn·*chees*·mahn?

¿Maykamataq
wichanchisman?

Is there a hut up there?
chookh·lyah *kahn*·choo
hah·*nahkh*·pee?

¿Chuklla kanchu
hanaqpi?

TREKKING

When does it get dark?
ee·mah oo·*rahs*·mee
too·*tah*·yahn?

¿Ima urasmi
tutayan?

Where can I hire mountain gear?
mai·*pee*·tahkh *or*·ko
wee·chah·*nah*·pahkh
ee·mah·*tah*·pahs
ahl·kee·lah·*rui*·mahn?

¿Maypitaq urqu
wichanapaq
imatapas
alkilarquyman?

Where can we buy supplies?
mai·*pee*·tahkh ee·mai·*mah*·nah
kahkh·koo·*nah*·tah
rahn·tee·rui·*koo*·mahn?

¿Maypitaq imaymana
kaqkunata
rantirquykuman?

Do you have llamas?
kahn·choo
lyah·mai·kee·*koo*·nah?

¿Kanchu
llamaykikuna?

How much do you charge for ...?	hai·*k'ah*·tahn koob·*rahn*·kee ...?	¿*Hayk'atan kubranki* ...?
a day	*sah*·pah *p'oon*·chai	*sapa p'unchay*
donkeys	ahs·nui·kee·koo·nah·*mahn*·tah	*asnuykikuna-manta*
llamas	lyah·mai·kee·koo·nah·*mahn*·tah	*llamaykikuna-manta*
mules	moo·lai·kee·koo·nah·*mahn*·tah	*mulaykikuna-manta*
a tent	kahr·pai·kee·*mahn*·tah	*karpaykimanta*

TREKKING

ON THE PATH

ÑANPI

Could you tell me the way to ...?
    mai·*teen*·tahn ...·mahn *reen*·chees?

¿*Maynintan* ...-*man rinchis?*

Does this path go to ...?
    ...·mahn *reen*·choo kai nyahn?

¿...-*man rinchu kay ñan?*

Where have you come from?
    mai·mahn·*tah*·tahkh hah·moo·*rahn*·kee?

¿*Maymantataq hamurqanki?*

How long did it take you?
    hai·k'ah p'oon·chai·*pee*·tahkh chah·yah·rah·*moon*·kee?

¿*Hayk'a p'unchaypitaq chayarqamunki?*

Where's the nearest village?
    mai·*pee*·tahkh *kah*·shahn lyoo·*mahn*·tah *ahs*·wahn *sees*·pah lyahkh·*tah*·kah?

¿*Maypitaq kashan lliwmanta aswan sispa llaqtaqa?*

Where can we spend the night?
    mai·*pee*·tahkh poo·nyoo·pah·koo·yoo·*kui*·mahn?

¿*Maypitaq puñupakuyukuyman?*

Can I leave some things here for a while?
    pahkh·tah rah·too·kah·*mah*·lyah k'e·pee·koo·*nah*·tah sah·ke·yoo·kui·*kee*·mahn kai·pee?

¿*Paqta ratukamalla q'ipikunata saqiyukuykiman kaypi?*

May I cross your property?
    chahk·*rai*·kekh keen·rai·*lyahn*·tah   *¿Chakraykiq*
    pah·sai·*mahn*·choo?   *kinrayllanta pasaymanchu?*
Can we go through here?
    kai·*neen*·tah   *¿Kayninta*
    poo·ree·koo·*mahm*·choo?   *puriykumanchu?*
Is this water OK to drink?
    ah·*lyeen*·choo   *¿Allinchu*
    ook·yah·*nah*·pahkh kai *oo*·noo?   *ukyanapaq kay unu?*
I'm lost.
    cheen·*kahs*·kahn poo·ree·*shah*·nee   *Chinkasqan purishani.*

altitude	*sah*·yai	*sayay*
altitude sickness	soo·*roo*·chee	*suruchi*
backpack	*k'e*·pee	*q'ipi*
candle	*bee*·lah	*bila*
to climb	wee·chai/*se*·kai	*wichay/siqay*
downhill	*oo*·rai	*uray*
first-aid kit	*hahm*·pee choo·*rah*·nah	*hampi churana*
gloves	*wahn*·tees	*wantis*
guide	poo·sahkh	*pusaq*
guided trek	poo·*sahkh*·wahn poo·ree	*pusaqwan puriy*
hike/to hike	*poo*·ree	*puriy*
hunting	*chah*·koo	*chaku*
hut	ch'ookh·lyah	*ch'uklla*
lookout	k-hah·*wah*·nah	*qhawana*
map	*mah*·pah	*mapa*
mountain climbing	or·ko wee·chai	*urqu wichay*
pick (tool)	*pee*·koo	*piku*
provisions (food)	*ko*·kow	*ququaw*
provisions (things)	kahkh·*koo*·nah	*kaqkuna*
rock climbing	kah·kah wee·chai	*qaqa wichay*
rope	*wahs*·k-hah	*waskha*
signpost	oo·*nahm*·chah	*unancha*
steep	*sah*·yahkh	*sayaq*
trek/to trek	*kah*·roo poo·ree	*karu puriy*
uphill	wee·chai/*hah*·nai	*wichay/hanay*
to walk	*poo*·ree	*puriy*

TREKKING

CAMPING

KARPA RUWAY

Designated camp sites exist only in tourist places like Machu Picchu or Sacsayhuamán. As long as you have permission from the locals, you can pitch your tent almost anywhere.

Is there a camp site nearby?
  kahn·choo *kai*·pee *pahm*·pah
  kahr·*pah*·pahkh?

¿Kanchu kaypi pampa karpapaq?

Can we camp here?
  kahr·*pah*·tah
  roo·wai·koo·*mahn*·choo
  kai·pee?

¿Karpata ruwaykumanchu kaypi?

Who owns this land?
  pekh·tahkh kai *chahkh*·rah?

¿Piqtaq kay chakra?

Can I talk to him/her?
  ree·mai·*mahn*·choo *pai*·wahn?

¿Rimaymanchu paywan?

Where can I hire a tent?
  mai·*pee*·tahkh kahr·*pah*·tah
  ahl·kee·lah·*rui*·mahn?

¿Maypitaq karpata alkilarquyman?

Are there shower facilities?
  kahn·choo *bah*·nyoo
  ahr·mah·koo·*nah*·pahkh?

¿Kanchu bañu armakunapaq?

blanket	*choo·see/ kah·*tah/ *mahn·*tah	*chusi/qata/* *manta*
camping	kahm·pah·*meen·*too	*kampamintu*
camp site	kahr·*pah·*pahkh *pahm·*pah	*karpapaq* *pampa*
firewood	*lyahn·*t'ah	*llant'a*
hammer	tah·*kah·*nah	*takana*
hammock	ah·*mah·*kah	*amaka*
knife	koo·*chee·*lyoo/ koo·*choo·*nah	*kuchillu/* *kuchuna*
matches	p-hoos·*poo·*roo	*phuspuru*
mattress (bedding)	poo·*nyoo·*nah	*puñuna*
rope	*wahs·*k-hah	*waskha*
sleeping bag	poo·*nyoo·*nah	*puñuna*
tent (pegs)	*kahr·*pah (tah·kahr·poo·*koo·*nah)	*karpa* *(takarpukuna)*
torch (flashlight)	k'ahn·*chah·*nah/ leen·*teer·*nah	*k'anchana/* *lintirna*
water	oo·noo/*yah·*koo	*unu/yaku*
water bottle	woo·*tee·*lyah oo·noo/*yah·*koo	*wutilla* *unu/yaku*

TREKKING

WEATHER   **PACHA/TIMPU**

What's the weather like?
ee·*mai·*nahn *pah·*chah/ *teem·*poo kah·shahn?	*¿Imaynan pacha/* *timpu kashan?*

What's the forecast for tomorrow?
ee·*mai·*nahn *pah·*chah/ *teem·*poo *kahn·*kah pah·*kah·*reen?	*¿Imaynan pacha/* *timpu kanqa* *paqarin?*

Today it's ...	...·shahn *koo·*nahn *p'oon·*chai	...*-shan kunan* *p'unchay.*
cold/chilly	*chee·*ree	*chiri*
hot/sunny	*roo·*p-hah	*rupha*
windy	*seen·*chee *wai·*rah	*sinchi wayra*

It's raining heavily.
　nee·*shoo*·tahn pah·*rah*·shahn　　*Nishutan parashan.*
It's raining lightly.
　pee·see·*lyah*·tahn pah·*rah*·shahn　*Pisillatan parashan.*
It's flooding.
　lyok·lyah·*shahn*·mee　　　　*Lluqllashanmi.*

TREKKING

cloud	*p-hoo*·yoo	*phuyu*
dew	*ch-hoo*·lyah	*chhulla*
drizzle	*ee*·p-hoo	*iphu*
dry season	*ch'ah*·kee *mee*·tah	*ch'aki mita*
fog/mist	*pah*·chah *p-hoo*·yoo	*pacha phuyu*
frost	*kah*·sah/*k-hoo*·pah	*qasa/qhupa*
glacier	*ree*·t'ee	*rit'i*
hail	*cheek*·chee	*chikchi*
hot	*roo*·p-hoo	*rupha*
ice	ch-hoo·*lyoon*·koo	*chhullunku*
lightning	ee·*lyah*·pah/	*illapa/*
	lyeef·*lyee*	*lliphlli*
rain	*pah*·rah	*para*
rainy season	*pah*·rai *mee*·tah	*paray mita*
shade	*lyahn*·t·hoo	*llanthu*
snow	*ree*·t'ee	*rit'i*
storm	*lyokh*·lyah *pah*·rah	*lluqlla para*
sun	*een*·tee	*inti*
sunny	*roo*·p-hah	*rupha*
thunder	*k-hahkh*·yah	*qhaqya*
warm	toom·pah·*lyah*·tah	*tumpallata*
	roo·p-hah	*rupha*
wind	*wai*·rah	*wayra*
windy	*seen*·chee *wai*·rah	*sinchi wayra*

GEOGRAPHICAL TERMS

PACHA SUTIKUNA

cave	*mah*·ch'ai	*mach'ay*
cliff	*kah*·kah	*qaqa*
earthquake	*pah*·chah *koo*·yui	*pacha kuyu*
forest	*mahly*·kee *mahly*·kee	*mallki mallki*
gap	*k'eekh*·lyoo	*k'ikllu*
high plateau	*poo*·nah/*sahly*·kah	*puna/sallqa*
hill	*or*·ko·chah/*mo*·ko	*urqucha/muqu*
hot spring	*k'o*·nee *pook*·yoo	*q'uñi pukyu*
hot valley	*yoon*·kah	*yunka*
lake	*ko*·chah	*qucha*
mountain	*or*·ko	*urqu*
mountain path	*or*·ko·pee nyahn	*urqupi ñan*
pass (narrow)	*k'ah*·sah	*q'asa*
peak	*or*·kohk *poon*·tahn	*urquq puntan*
ravine	*wai*·k'o	*wayq'u*
river	*mah*·yoo	*mayu*
sea	*ko*·chah·*mah*·mah	*quchamama*
snow line	*ree*·t'ee *se*·ke	*riti siqi*
stone/rock	*roo*·mee/*wahn*·k'ah	*rumi/wank'a*
volcano	*nee*·nah p·*hokh*·chekh *or*·ko	*nina phuqchiq urqu*
waterfall	p·*hahkh*·chah/p·*how*·chee	*phaqcha/phawchi*

TREKKING

FAUNA　　　　　　IMAYMANA ANIMALKUNA

What animal is that?

　　ee·mah ah·nee·*mahl*·tahkh chai?　　*¿Ima animaltaq chay?*

Domestic Creatures　　　　　　Uywakuna

alpaca	ahl·*pah*·kah	*alpaka*
cat	mee·see/*mee*·chee	*misi/michi*
dog	*ahl*·ko/*aly*·ko	*alqu/allqu*
donkey	*ahs*·noo	*asnu*
goat	*kow*·rah	*kawra*
horse	kah·*wah*·lyoo	*kawallu*
guanaco	wah·*nah*·koo	*wanaku*
(like a llama)		
llama	*lyah*·mah	*llama*
mule	*moo*·lah	*mula*
ox	*too*·roo	*turu*
pig	k·*hoo*·chee	*khuchi*
sheep	*ook*·yah/oo·*wee*·hah	*ukya/uwiha*

Birds　　　　　　Pisqukuna

Andean flamingo	pah·ree·*wah*·nah	*pariwana*
Andean songbird	*poo*·kui *poo*·kui	*pukuy pukuy*
condor	*koon*·toor	*kuntur*
wild duck	*choo*·lyoo *mah*·yoo	*chullu mayu*
eagle	*ahn*·kah	*anka*
falcon/hawk	*wah*·mahn	*waman*
hummingbird	(ko·ree) *k'en*·tee	*(quri) q'inti*
owl	*too*·koo/*hoo*·koo	*tuku/huku*
partridge	*yoo*·t·hoo/*lyoo*·t·hoo	*yuthu/lluthu*
rooster	*k'ahn*·kah	*k'anka*
seagull	*kely*·wah/*kyoo*·lyah/	*qillwa/qiwlla/*
	kely·*wai*·too	*qillwaytu*
sparrowhawk	*ahn*·kah/*wah*·mahn	*anka/waman*
turtledove	*kooly*·koo	*kullku*
vulture	soo·we·*k'ah*·rah	*suwiq'ara*
woodpecker	hah·*k'ahkh*·lyoo	*hak'akllu*

TREKKING

Wildlife · Salqa Animalkuna

armadillo	keer·*keen*·choo	*kirkinchu*
bear	oo·*koo*·koo	*ukuku*
deer	tah·*roo*·kah	*taruka*
fish	*chahly*·wah	*challwa*
fox	*ah*·tokh	*atuq*
frog	hahm·*p'ah*·too	*hamp'atu*
game (animals)	chah·koo·*nah*·pahkh	*chakunapaq*
	ah·nee·mahl·*koo*·nah	*animalkuna*
leech	*yah*·wahr ch'on·kahkh	*yawar ch'unqaq*
lizard	soo·koo·*lyoo*·koo/	*sukulluku/*
	kah·*rai*·wah	*qaraywa*
monkey	koo·*see*·lyoo	*kusillu*
mountain lion	*poo*·mah	*puma*
snake	mah·*ch'ahkh*·wai/	*mach'aqway/*
	ah·*mah*·roo	*amaru*
spider	ah·*rah*·nyah;	*araña;*
	koo·see·*koo*·see	*kusi-kusi*
trout	*troo*·chah	*trucha*
turtle	chah·*rah*·pah	*charapa*
vicuña	wee·*k'oo*·nyah	*wik'uña*
(like a llama)		
viscacha (rodent)	wees·*k'ah*·chah	*wisk'acha*
wildcat	os·*k-ho*·lyoo	*usqhullu*
wild pig	see·*wai*·roo	*siwayru*

Insects · Kuru

bee	lah·*chee*·wah	*lachiwa*
butterfly	peely·*peen*·too	*pillpintu*
cockroach	koo·kah·*rah*·chah	*kukaracha*
dung beetle	*ah*·kah *tahn*·kah	*aka tanqa*
flea	*pee*·kee	*piki*
fly	ch'oos·pee	*ch'uspi*
louse/lice	*oo*·sah/oo·sah·*koo*·nah	*usa/usakuna*
mosquito	*k-he*·te *(ch'oos*·pee)	*qhiti (ch'uspi)*

TREKKING

TREKKING

THE LEGEND OF THE INCAS

At the beginning of time, near Lake Titicaca high in the Peruvian Andes, in a place known as *Paqariqtampu*, pah·kah·rekh·*tahm*·poo, there appeared four brothers and four sisters, who were all children of the Sun, the highest of deities. The Sun charged these brothers and sisters with teaching humankind the principles of civilization, truth and justice. For this purpose, he gave them a golden staff, with which they were to seek out the ideal site to found an empire. They would know this site when the staff was swallowed up completely by the earth, upon striking the ground.

The brothers and sisters began their search for an empire by first organising the people living around Paqariqtampu into *ayllus*, ai·lyoos, or communities. They taught the people to cultivate the land, weave fibres and build houses; about laws, wars and the religion of the Sun. After this, everyone departed in search of their promised land, and *Manqu Khapaq*, *mahn*·ko k-hah·pahkh, and *Mama Uqllu*, *mah·mah okh*·lyo, the principal figures of the divine family, struck the ground every day with the magic staff. Finally, they arrived near a hill called Wanakawri, wah·nah·*kow*·ree, where, with the first strike, the golden staff disappeared. *Manqu Khapaq* and *Mama Uqllu* decided to establish the city of Qusqu, *kos*·ko, or 'Cuzco', which became the centre of their empire, Tawantinsuyu, *tah·wahn·teen·soo·yoo*, meaning 'four parts or regions (of the empire)'.

FLORA & AGRICULTURE
Trees, Plants & Flowers

MALLKI MALLKIPAS CHAKRA RURUPAS
Sach'akunapas Yurakunapas

What ... is that?	*ee*·mah ... chai?	¿Ima ... chay?
tree	sah·*ch'ah*·tahkh	sach'ataq
plant	yoo·*rah*·tahkh	yurataq
flower	t'ee·*kah*·tahkh	t'ikataq
agave (aloe)	*pahkh*·pah	paqpa
broom (bush)	*t'ahn*·kahr	t'anqar
cactus	*k'ahkh*·lyah/	k'aklla/
	ah·nyah·*pahn*·koo	añapanku
cactus fruit	*too*·nahs	tunas
coca	*koo*·kah	kuka
eucalyptus	yoo·kah·*leekh*·too	yukaliptu
medlar	wees·*wee*·roo	wiswiru
mountain grass	*ee*·ch·hoo	ichhu
nettle	*kee*·sah/*k'oo*·rah	kisa/k'ura
pine	*pee*·noo	pinu
quingual (Andean tree)	*keen*·wahl	kinwal
scrub	*ch'ah*·p-hrah	ch'aphra
thorn/spine	*kees*·kah	kiska
totora reed	t'oo·*too*·rah	t'utura
white poplar	*kees*·wahr	kiswar
wild cherry tree	kah·*poo*·lee	kapuli

Herbs & Crops

Qurakunapis, Rurukunapis

beans	ahl·*weer*·hahs	alwirhas
cabbage	*koo*·lees	kulis
coriander *(cilantro)*	koo·*lahn*·troo	kulantru
corn	*sah*·rah	sara
fava beans	*hah*·wahs	hawas
flower	t'ee·kah/*wai*·tah	t'ika/wayta

TREKKING

TREKKING

garlic	*ah·*hoos	*ahus*
huacatay (aromatic herb)	wah·*kah·*tai	*wakatay*
kiwicha (grain)	kee·*wee·*chah	*kiwicha*
leaf	*rah·*p-hee/*rah·*p'ah	*raphi/rap'a*
lemon tree	*lee·*moon *sah·*ch'ah	*limun sach'a*
lupine	*tahr·*wee	*tarwi*
mashua (local tuber)	*ah·*nyoo/*mahs·*wah	*añu/maswa*
oca (tuber)	*o·*kah	*uqa*
onion	see·*wee·*lyah	*siwilla*
orange tree	lah·*rahn·*hah *sah·*ch'ah	*laranha sach'a*
orchard	*moo·*yah	*muya*
papaya (highland)	pah·*pah·*yah	*papaya*
parsley	pee·*ree·*heel	*pirihil*
peas	ahl·*weer·*hahs	*alwirhas*
potatoes	*pah·*pah	*papa*
quinoa	*kyoo·*nah/*kyoo·*nyah	*kiwna/kiwña*
tree	*mahly·*kee	*mallki*
wheat	*tree·*yoo	*triyu*
yacón (tuber)	*lyah·*kom/*yah·*koo	*llaqum/yaku*

Use Quechua for building a rapport with market vendors.

LOOKING FOR ...   ... MASKHAY

Where's a/the nearest ...?	mai·*pee*·tahkh ... kahn?	¿Maypitaq ... kan?
bank	*kol·*ke *wah*·see	qulqi wasi
market	k-*hah*·too	qhatu
music shop	moo·*see*·kah teen·dah	musika tinda
pharmacy	hahm·*pee*·yokh wah·see	hampiyuq wasi
shoe shop	sah·*pah*·too teen·dah	sapatu tinda
shop	*teen*·dah	tinda

Where can I buy (a) ...?	mai·*pee*·tahkh ... rahn·tee·*rui*·mahn?	¿Maypitaq ... rantirquyman?
book	lyoo·roo·koo·*nah*·tah	liwrukunata
clothes	p'ah·chah·koo·*nah*·tah	p'achakunata
handicrafts	ahr·tee·sah·nee·yah·koo·*nah*·tah	artisaniyakunata
souvenirs	*too*·kui *reek*·ch'ahkh ee·mai·mah·nah·koo·*nah*·tah	tukuy rikch'aq imaymanakunata

Where can I get a haircut?
mai·*pee*·tahkh chook·*chai*·tah
roo·too·chee·koo·*rui*·mahn?
¿Maypitaq chukchayta rutuchikurquyman?

MAKING A PURCHASE   RANTIY

I'd like to buy ...
...·tah rahn·*tee*·tahn
moo·*nai*·mahn
...-ta rantiytan munayman.

I'm just looking.
k-hah·*wai*·lyahn
k-hah·wah·*shah*·nee
Qhawayllan qhawashani.

Can you write down the price?
chah·*neen*·tah
kel·kahn·kee·*mahn*·choo?
¿Chaninta qilqankimanchu?

Can I look at it?
k·hah·wai·kui·*mahn*·choo?   *¿Qhawaykuymanchu?*

Do you have any others?
hokh·*koo*·nah   *¿Huqkuna*
kah·poo·soon·*kee*·choo?   *kapusunkichu?*

I don't like it.
mah·nahn *kai*·tah   *Manan kayta*
moo·nah·*nee*·choo   *munanichu.*

OK, I'll buy it.
ah·lyeen,·mee *chai*·tah   *Allinmi, chayta*
ah·pah·*koo*·sahkh/   *apakusaq/rantisaq.*
rahn·*tee*·sahkh

How much is it all together?
hai·k'ahn lyoo·neen·koo?   *¿Hayk'an lliwninku?*

Could I have a receipt please?
ree·see·*woo*·tah   *¿Risiwuta*
ko·wahn·kee·*mahn*·choo?   *quwankimanchu?*

I want to exchange this.
kai·tah kahm·bee·*yai*·tah   *Kayta kambiyayta*
moo·*nah*·nee   *munani.*

It's faulty.
mah·nahn kai ah·*lyeen*·choo   *Manan kay allinchu.*

I'd like my money back.
kol·*kee*·tah koo·tee·chee·*poo*·wai   *Qulqiyta kutichipuway.*

THEY MAY SAY ...

yow *(tai*·tah *reen*·goo; *mah*·mah *reen*·gah)!
Listen (Sir/Madam)!

ee·mah·lyah·*tah*·pahs rahn·*tee*·wai, tai·*tai*/mah·*mai*
Please buy something from me, Sir/Madam.

hai·*k'ah*·tahn moo·*nahn*·kee?
How much/many do you want?

chah·*neen*·tah pee·see·yah·*chee*·sahkh *ree*·kee
I'll lower the price for you.

SHOPPING

BARGAINING   CHANINTA PISIYACHIY

Bargaining is a widespread practice in Latin America, especially in Peru. You can bargain for just about anything, except perhaps your bill at a fine restaurant or the cost of something at a department store. You'll definitely be expected to bargain with street or market sellers.

How much is this?
hai·*k'ah*·tahk chai?   ¿*Hayk'ataq chay?*

Really?
che·*kahkh*·choo?   ¿*Chiqaqchu?*

The price is too high.
seen·chee chah·nee·*yokh*·mee chai   *Sinchi chaniyuqmi chay.*

It's too much for me.
mah·nahn *kol*·kay   *Manan qulqiy*
ai·pah·*wahn*·choo   *aypawanchu.*

Can you lower the price?
chah·*neen*·tah   ¿*Chaninta*
pee·see·yah·cheen·kee·*mahn*·choo/   *pisiyachinkimanchu/*
oo·rai·kah·cheen·kee·*mahn*·choo?   *uraykachinkimanchu?*

Do you have something cheaper?
mah·nah *ahm*·chah chah·nee·yokh   ¿*Mana ancha chaniyuq*
ee·mah·lyai·*kee*·pahs   *imallaykipas*
kah·poo·soon·*kee*·choo?   *kapusunkichu?*

Is that your final price?
chai·choo chah·*neen* ree·kee?   ¿*Chaychu chanin riki?*

I'll give you ...
...·tah koy·koo·*sai*·kee   ...*-ta quykusayki.*

SOUVENIRS   **IMAYMANAKUNA**
                       RANTINAPAQ

baskets	ai·sah·nah·*koo*·nah/	*aysanakuna/*
	p'ookh·too·*koo*·nah/	*p'uktukuna/*
	kah·nahs·tah·*koo*·nah	*kanastakuna*
handicrafts	ahr·tee·sah·nee·yah·*koo*·nah	*artisaniyakuna*
jewellery	ee·lyah/oo·*mee*·nyah	*illa/umiña*

SHOPPING

masks	oo·yah·tee·*koo*·nah	*uyatikuna*
musical	moo·*see*·kah	*musika*
instruments	wah·kah·chee·nah·*koo*·nah	*waqachinakuna*
pottery	*rahkh*·cheel/*k'ahkh*·rah	*raqchi/k'akra*
shell souvenirs	ch'oo·roo·*mahn*·tah	*ch'urumanta*
	roo·*wahs*·kah	*ruwasqa*
	ee·mah·mai·nah·*koo*·nah	*imamaynakuna*
tapestries	t'e·ke·*koo*·nah	*t'iqikuna*
wood carvings	k'oo·lyoo·*mahn*·tah	*k'ullumanta*
	roo·*wahs*·kah	*ruwasqa*
	reekh·ch'ay	*rikch'ay*
woven textiles	ah·wai·*koo*·nah	*awaykuna*

CLOTHING   P'ACHA

bag	wah·*yah*·kah	*wayaqa*
belt (Andean)	*choom*·pee	*chumpi*
blanket	*kah*·tah/*choo*·see/	*qata/chusi/*
boots	*boo*·tahs	*butas*
cap (Andean)	ch'oo·lyoo	*ch'ullu*
dress	*p'ah*·chah	*p'acha*
handbag	*ch'oos*·pah	*ch'uspa*
hat	soom·*ree*·roo	*sumriru*
jacket	*sah*·koo	*saku*
jeans	pahn·*tah*·loon	*pantalun*
jumper (sweater)	*choom*·pah	*chumpa*
poncho	*poon*·choo	*punchu*
purse	*ch'oos*·pah	*ch'uspa*
scarf	chah·*lee*·nah	*chalina*
shawl	*lyeekh*·lyah	*lliklla*
shirt	kah·*mee*·sah	*kamisa*
shoes	sah·pah·too·*koo*·nah	*sapatukuna*
skirt	poo·*lyee*·rah	*pullira*
socks	*mee*·dyahs	*midyas*
T-shirt	*oon*·k·hoo/	*unkhu/*
	kah·mee·*see*·tah	*kamisita*

SHOPPING

Can I try it on?
| choo·rah·kui·koo·*mahn*·choo *chai*·tah? | ¿Churakuykumanchu chayta? |

It doesn't fit.
| *mah*·nahn sah·yai·*nee*·choo | Manan sayayniychu. |

It's too ...	*kai*·kah ....mee/·n	Kayqa ...-mil-n.
big	*hah*·toon	hatun
large	*seen*·chee *hah*·toon	sinchi hatun
long	*wahs*·k'ah	wask'a
small	*hoo*·chui	huchuy
short	*teen*·koo/ *tahkh*·sah	tinku/taksa
tight	*k'ees*·kee	k'iski

MATERIALS   IMATAPAS RUWANAPAQ

bamboo	to·*ko*·ro/ *so*·kos	tuquru/suqus
bone	*too*·lyoo	tullu
ceramic	*rahkh*·chee/ *k'ahkh*·rah	raqch'i/k'akra
clay	*lyahn*·k'ee/ *lyeen*·k'ee	llank'i/llink'i
cotton	*oot*·k-hoo	utkhu
handmade	mah·*kee*·wahn	makiwan
	roo·*wahs*·kah	ruwasqa
fabric	*lyee*·kah/ *ah*·wah	llika/awa
glass	*kes*·pee	qispi
gold	*ko*·ree	quri
horn	*wahkh*·rah	waqra
leather	*kah*·rah	qara
metal	*ahm*·tah/ *tee*·tee	anta/titi
plastic	plahs·*tee*·koo	plastiku
reed	so·kos/ *k'oor*·koor	suqus/k'urkur
silver	*kol*·ke	qulqi
stainless steel	ah·*see*·roo	asiru
stone	*roo*·mee	rumi
straw	*ee*·ch-hoo	ichhu
thread	*k'ai*·too	q'aytu
wood	*k'oo*·lyoo	k'ullu
wool	*meely*·mah/ *meely*·wah	millma/millwa

SHOPPING

SHOPPING

COLOURS
LLIMP'IKUNA

black	*yah*·nah	*yana*
blue	*ahn*·kahs/*ah*·sool	*anqas/asul*
brown	*ch'oom*·pee	*ch'umpi*
colour	*lyeem*·p'ee/*koo*·loor/	*llimp'i/kulur/*
	tooly·pee	*tullpi*
green	*k'o*·mer	*q'umir*
grey	*o*·ke/*ch'ekh*·chee/*tee*·tee	*uqi/ch'iqchi/titi*
orange	wee·*lah*·pee	*wilapi*
pink	*pahm*·tee;	*panti;*
	lyahm·k-hah *poo*·kah	*llanqha puka*
purple	*koo*·lyee/*moo*·*rah*·roo	*kulli/muraru*
red	*poo*·kah	*puka*
white	*yoo*·rahkh	*yuraq*
yellow	*k'e*·lyoo	*q'illu*

WOOLLY LOGIC

In the Andes, several wool-producing animals have been domesticated and are clipped for their wool. These include alpacas *(alpaka,* ahl·*pah*·kah), guanacos *(wanaku,* wah·*nah*·koo) sheep *(ukya/uwiha,* ook·yah/oo·*wee*·hah) and llamas *(llama, lyah*·mah). The alpaca-like vicuña *(wik'uña,* wee·*k'oo*·nyah), an undomesticated species, was once hunted for its wool, but it's now considered endangered. No matter what its source, the word for wool in Quechua is *millma, meely*·mah, or its variant, *millwa, meely*·wah.

Wool can be used to make a range of clothing and accessories which traditionally exhibit a variety of regional motifs *(pallay, pah*·lyai). Common designs include coca and potato flowers, llamas, alpacas and vicuñas, mountains, cacti, the Inca figure, masks, patterns of multi-coloured lines, birds, and silhouettes of towns and people working or socialising.

TOILETRIES   SUMAQYACHIQKUNA

comb	*nyahkh·*ch'ah	*ñaqch'a*
razor	*soon·*k-hah roo·*too·*nah/	*sunkha rutuna/*
	k'ee·*soo·*nah	*k'isuna*
shampoo	*chahm·*poo	*champu*
soap	*hah·*woon	*hawun*
tissues	*sen·*kah pee·*chah·*nah	*sinqa pichana*
toothbrush	*kee·*roo k-he·*too·*nah	*kiru qhituna*

FOR THE BABY   WAWACHAPAQ

baby powder	wah·*wah·*pahkh *tahl·*koo	*wawapaq talku*
bib	bah·*bee·*roo	*babiru*
bottle	bee·*bee·*roon	*bibirun*
nappies/diapers	ah·kah·*wah·*rah/	*akawara/*
	wahl·*t'ah·*nah	*walt'ana*
dummy/pacifier	nyoo·*nyoo·*nah	*ñuñuna*
teat	*nyoo·*nyoo	*ñuñu*

SMOKING   PITAY

Smoking is much more common among men than women; traditionally, it's unacceptable for women to smoke. As times have changed, some women have taken it up, especially the *hampiq*, *hahm·*pekh, or folk healers. You should ask if it's OK to light up when in close proximity to others.

Do you sell cigarettes here?
  see·yah·roo·koo·*nah·*tah   *¿Siyarukunata*
  been·deen·*kee·*choo?   *bindinkichu?*
Do you smoke?
  pee·tahn·*kee·*choo kahn?   *¿Pitankichu qan?*
Do you have a light?
  foos·poo·*rui·*kee *kahn·*choo?   *¿Phuspuruyki kanchu?*
Do you mind if I smoke?
  pee·tai·*mahn·*choo *kai·*pee?   *¿Pitaymanchu kaypi?*
Please don't smoke.
  ah·*lyee·*choo *ah·*mah pee·*tai·*choo   *Allichu ama pitaychu.*

SHOPPING

cigarettes	see·*yah*·roo	*siyaru*
cigars	*hah*·toon ch'oom·pee	*hatun ch'umpi*
	see·*yah*·roo	*siyaru*
lighter	*nee*·nah rah·tah·*chee*·nah;	*nina ratachina;*
	k'ahn·chah·*chee*·nah	*k'anchachina*
matches	foos·*poo*·roo	*phuspuru*
tobacco	tah·*wah*·koo	*tawaku*

SIZES & COMPARISONS — SAYAYKUNAPAS TINKUCHIKUYKUNAPAS

a little bit	pee·see·*lyah*·tah/	*pisillata/*
	toom·pah·*lyah*·tah	*tumpallata*
also	....pees/·pahs	*...-pis/-pas*
big	*hah*·toon	*hatun*
enough	chai·*lyah*·nyah	*chayllaña*
heavy	*lyah*·sahkh	*llasaq*
light	*ch-hah*·lyah	*chhalla*
little (amount)	*pee*·see/*toom*·pah	*pisi/tumpa*
many	*ahs*·k·hah/*ch-hee*·kah	*askha/chhika*
more	*ahs*·wahn	*aswan*
small	*hoo*·chui	*huchuy*
too much/ many	*ahs*·k·hah *ahs*·k·hah; *ch-hee*·kah *ch-hee*·kah	*askha askha; chhika chhika*

A great variety of dishes and cuisine is available throughout the Andes. In most restaurants, staff will speak Spanish, so Quechua will be more useful for visits to local markets, fairs, festivals and small restaurants.

THROUGH THE DAY   P'UNCHAYNINTIN

Since rural Andeans rise with the sun, breakfast may be as early as five or six o'clock in the morning. Lunch, the biggest meal of the day, is at midday, while dinner is around six in the evening. Bedtime is generally at nightfall. This routine varies for festivals and holidays, when everyone has a chance to party.

breakfast	*mah·*tee; *oo·*noo *k'o·*nyee	*mati; unu q'uñi*
lunch	*ahl·moo·*sai/*mee·*k-hui	*almusay/mikhuy*
dinner	*too·*tah *mee·*k-hui; *see·*nah	*tuta mikhuy; sina*

SPECIAL   QHALI KAYPAQ
DIETS   MIKHUYKUNA

Meat is an integral part of the Andean diet, even though it may be served in small quantities. You won't find vegetarian meals in small rural restaurants or when staying at someone's home.

Does this dish have meat in it?
    ai·chah·*yokh·*choo kai
    mee·*k-hoo·*nah?   *¿Aychayuqchu kay*
                              mikhuna?
Can I get this without meat?
    *mah·*nah ai·chah·*yohkh·*tah
    kah·rai·koo·wahn·kee·*mahm·*choo   *¿Mana aychayuqta*
    *kai·*tah?   *qaraykuwankimanchu*
                              kayta?

FOOD

133

I don't eat meat.
mah·nahn ai·*chah*·tah	*Manan aychata*
mee·k-hoo·*nee*·choo	*mikhunichu.*

I don't eat chicken or fish.
mah·nahn *wahly*·pah ai·*chah*·tah,	*Manan wallpa aychata,*
chahly·wah ai·*chah*·tah	*challwa aychata*
mee·k-hoo·*nee*·choo	*mikhunichu.*

I can't eat dairy products.
mah·nah lee·chee·*mahn*·tah	*Manan lichimanta*
roo·*wahs*·kah	*ruwasqa*
mee·k-hui·koo·*nah*·tah	*mikhuykunata*
mee·*k-hui*·tah ah·tee·*nee*·choo	*mikhuyta atinichu.*

Does it contain egg?
roon·too·*yohkh*·choo *kai*·kah?	*¿Runtuyuqchu kayqa?*

I'm allergic to (peanuts).
mah·nahn (mah·*nee*)·tah	*Manan (mani)-ta*
mee·k-hoo·*nee*·choo.	*mikhunichu.*
ah·leer·*hee*·koon kah·nee	*Alirhikun kani.*

EATING OUT   MIKHUNA WASIPIPAS KARPAPIPAS MIKHUY

Eating out in rural areas means eating communally outdoors during festivals, fairs or Sunday market days. Local dishes are easily found in *chicherías*, or chicha bars – *aqha wasikuna*, *ah*·khah wah·see·*koo*·nah – and *picanterías*, inexpensive restaurants specialising in spicy dishes. For particularly spicy food, try dishes labelled *arequipeña*, 'Arequipa style', or *a la criolla*, 'Creole style'.

Is there anything to eat?
kahn·choo ee·mah·*lyah*·pahs	*¿Kanchu imallapas*
mee·k-hoo·*nah*·pahkh?	*mikhunapaq?*

Yes, there is.
ah·*ree,* kahn·mee	*Arí, kanmi.*

No, there isn't.
mah·nahn *kahn*·choo	*Manan kanchu.*

Could you recommend something?
ee·mah·*tah*·tahkh
mee·k·hoo·*rui*·mahn?

*¿Imatataq
mikhurquyman?*

Is there any salad?
een·sah·*lah*·dah *kahn*·choo?

¿Insalada kanchu?

I'll have what they're having.
pai·*koo*·nah
mee·k·hoo·shahn·*koo*·tah
no·*kah*·pahs moo·*nah*·nee

*Paykuna
mikhushankuta
nuqapas munani.*

What's in that dish?
ee·mah·*yokh*·mee chai
mee·*k·hoo*·nah?

*¿Imayuqmi chay
mikhuna?*

COMPLIMENTS TO THE CHEF

I love this dish.
kai mee·k·hoo·*nah*·tah
ahn·*chah*·tah moo·*nah*·nee

*Kay mikhunata
anchata munani.*

I'm satisfied/full.
sahkh·*sahs*·kah *kah*·nee

Saksasqa kani.

We love the local cuisine.
kai lyahkh·*tah*·pee
mee·k·hoo·*nah*·tah
seen·*chee*·tah moo·*nai*·koo

*Kay llaqtapi
mikhunata
sinchita munayku.*

That was delicious!
soo·mahkh mee·*k·hoo*·nah!

¡Sumaq mikhuna!

You're an excellent cook.
koo·sah wai·*k'okh*·mee
kahn·kee

*Kusa wayk'uqmi
kanki.*

FOOD

I want cold/hot water please.

ah·*lyee*·choo *chee*·ree/*k'o*·nyee		*Allichu chiri/q'uñi*
oo·*noo*·tah moo·*nah*·nee		*unuta munani.*

May I have some more please?

ah·*lyee*·choo		*Allichu*
yah·pah·yoo·wahn·*kee*·mahn		*yapayuwankiman.*

Please give	ah·*lyee*·choo ....tah	*Allichu ...-ta*
me a/an/the ...	*ko*·wai	*quway.*
ashtray	*oosh*·pah choo·*rah*·nah	*ushpa churana*
bill	*kween*·tah	*kwinta*
cup	*sui*·k'oo/	*suyk'u/*
	chui·*k'oo*·chah/	*chuyk'ucha/*
	poo·koo	*puku*
fork	tee·*nee*·roor	*tinirur*
knife	koo·*chee*·lyoo	*kuchillu*
plate	*p'oo*·koo/p'oo·*koo*·chah	*p'uku/p'ukucha*
pot	*mahn*·kah	*manka*
spoon	koo·*chah*·rah	*kuchara*
water	oo·*noo*/*yah*·koo	*unu/yaku*

to boil	t'eem·*poo*·chee	*t'impuchiy*
boiled	t'eem·*poos*·kah	*t'impusqa*
bread (stale)	*choo*·choo *t'ahn*·tah	*chuchu t'anta*
clean (things)	leem·*pee*·yoo/*lui*·loo	*limpiyu/luylu*
clean (water)	*ch'oo*·yah	*ch'uya*
cold	*chee*·ree	*chiri*
to cook	*wai*·k'ui	*wayk'uy*
cooked	chah·*yahs*·kah	*chayasqa*

FOOD

dirty	k-he·lyee/k-hahr·kah	qhilli/kharka
fresh (vegetables)	lyan·lyah	llanlla
greasy/fatty	wee·rah·sah·pah	wirasapa
to heat	k'o·nyee·chee	q'uñichiy
hot (temperature)	k'o·nyee	q'uñi
increase/addition	yah·pah	yapa
meat	(see·k'ah) ai·chah	(siq'a) aycha
raw	hahn·koo/chah·wah	hanku/chawa
to salt	kah·chee·chai	kachichay
salty	kah·chee·sah·pah	kachisapa
sour	p'os·ko	p'usqu
spicy	hah·yah	haya
stale/spoiled	mah·k'ah	maq'a
sweet	mees·k'ee	misk'i
to sweeten	mees·k'ee·chee	misk'ichiy
tart	k-hahkh·tee/lyo·ke	qhaqti/lluqi
to taste	mah·lyee	malliy
thick	t-hah·kah	thaka
watery	yah·koo·sah·pah	yakusapa

ANDEAN COOK-OUTS

In many rural regions, midday meals for special occasions and celebrations are still prepared in a cooking pit, or *pachamanka*, pah·chah·mahn·kah. A hole is dug and a small 'house' of stones constructed over it. A fire is built inside the 'house', heating the stones until they're white-hot, at which point they're tumbled into the hole. Meats, tubers, vegetables, tamales (meat parcels), grains and herbs are sandwiched between the layers of hot rock. Finally, the oven is sealed shut with herbs and large leaves to keep soil from falling through into the food, and covered with earth to seal in the heat until it's cooked to perfection. Meals are served sitting in a circle on the ground and are eaten as finger food.

FOOD

ANDEAN STAPLE DISHES
LLAQTANCHISPA MIKHUNAN

These are typical dishes that tend to be served every day, with little variation. Each region has its specialities but some dishes are common throughout the Andes:

chokh·lyo wai·k'oo   *chuqllu wayk'u*

  corn on the cob – available from March through to May, it's boiled and served with a kind of unripened cheese

choo·pee   *chupi*

  soup made from a variety of regional ingredients

ch'oo·nyoo   *ch'uñu*

  dried potatoes, *ch'arki*, *ch'ahr·kee*, and dried meat – similar to jerky – prepared with aromatic herbs

hah·k'oo/mahch·kah   *hak'u/machka*

  a flour made of any of a variety of grains (wheat, barley, quinoa or *cañihua*; or dried beans or peas)

hahn·k'ah/hahm·kah/   *hank'a/hamka/kamcha*
kahm·chah

  popcorn made from large kernels and served with a dry, cheddar-like cheese. The corn is toasted – or 'popped' – inside a *k'allana*, *k'ah·lyah·nah*, a low, open clay pot, and is put inside a clay oven known as a *q'uncha*, *k'on·chah*, or *tullpa*, *tooly·pah*.

moo·tee   *mut'i*

  dried corn kernels, boiled. A part of every corn harvest is set aside for drying, to be added to soup or ground into flour.

oo·choo koo·tah   *uchu kuta*

  hot pepper paste, that accompanies varieties of tuber

p·hoos·poo/poos·poo   *phuspu/puspu*

  dried beans (though can be fresh in season) reconstituted by boiling. All boiled foods are prepared in a clay pot known as a *manka*, *mahn·kah*.

FOOD

REGIONAL SPECIALITIES
WAKIN LLAQTAKUNAQ MIKHUNAN

Note the Spanish influence in the names of many dishes.

Argentina

em·pah·*nah*·dahs   *empanadas* (Spanish)
puff pastries filled with minced meat and spices and other ingredients served with *ruqru*, *rokh*·roo, a stew

Bolivia

ch'oo·nyoo   *ch'uñu*
freeze-dried potatoes, soaked overnight and then boiled to accompany main dishes

em·pah·*nah*·dahs   *empanadas salteñas* (Spanish)
sahl·*te*·nyahs
a type of meat pie

hahly·pah·*wai*·kah   *hallpawayka*
sauce made from tomatoes, fresh peppers and herbs

pe·*kah*·nah   *pecana* (Spanish)
traditional Christmas dish of beef or veal cooked in wine and herbs

pee·ke *mah*·cho   *pique macho* (Spanish)
beef grilled with hot peppers, chopped potatoes and onions and served with fried potatoes and gravy, or with *saqta de pollo*

sahkh·tah de po·lyo   *saqta de pollo*
chicken stew with peppers and onions

seel·*pahn*·cho   *silpancho cochabambino*
co·chah·bahm·*bee*·no
meat and egg dish covered with hot sauce

teem·poo   *timpu*
lamb stew

troo·chah   *trucha*
trout, a Lake Titicaca speciality

toon·tah   *tunta*
a type of freeze-dried potato, paler than the *ch'uñu*

FOOD

Colombia

hoo·*meen*·t'ah   *humint'a*
  pork, vegetable and rice tamale, wrapped in banana
  leaves and steamed
ko·wee   *quwi*
  grilled guinea pig

Ecuador

cahl·do de *pah*·tahs   *caldo de patas* (Spanish)
  soup made with cow hooves
se·*vee*·che de cah·mah·*ron*   *ceviche de camarón*
  a type of shrimp cocktail   (Spanish)
free·*tah*·dah   *fritada* (Spanish)
  small pieces of fried pork, served with *muti*, fried
  bananas, potatoes and hot peppers
lyah·*peen*·*gah*·choo   *llapingachu*
  potato-based dish, like a potato pancake
lo·cro de *pah*·pah   *locro de papa*
  potato and cheese soup
po·lyo seen *po*·lyo   *pollo sin pollo* (Spanish)
  'chicken without chicken', a vegetarian dish common
  to Quito, Otavalo and Baños
se·co de *chee*·vo   *seco de chivo* (Spanish)
  goat stew served with rice

Peru

Ancash

hah·kah *chahs*·kee   *haka chaski*
  guinea pig soup
pah·pah *chahs*·kee   *papa chaski*
  potato soup made with milk and cottage cheese
pe·*cahn cahl*·do   *pecán caldo* (Spanish)
  lamb's head broth
roo·*roo hee*·lyee   *ruru hilli*
  fruit punch made with local seasonal fruits

FOOD

*wahly·*pah *chahs·*kee   *wallpa chaski*
  chicken broth with peanuts and almonds

*yoo·*kah *shoo·*pee   *yuka shupi*
  low-fat soup served the morning after a late night

Arequipa

*choo·*pee de cah·*mah·ro·*nes   *chupi de camarones*
  prawn soup

*pahn·*kah *oo·*choo   *panka uchu*
  a special form of the ever-present ground hot pepper

*ro·*co·to re·*lye·*no   *rocoto relleno* (Spanish)
  a variety of stuffed hot peppers

Ayacucho

ah·*roo·*woo   *aruwu*
  meat stew (most often pork)

chee·*chah·*roo   *chicharu*
  fried shredded pork and potatoes

*kahn·*kah   *kanka*
  roast beef sauteed with onions, garlic, hot peppers
  and spices

moon·*doon·*goo   *mundungu*
  thick, rich soup made with beef, lamb or pork, usually
  including the tripe

pah·*tah·*chee   *patachi*
  thick soup made with barley and bacon

poo·*chee·*roo/*teem·*poo   *puchiru/timpu*
  thick soup of varying meats, tubers, legumes and rice

*poo·*kah pee·*kahn·*tee   *puka pikanti*
  spicy stew based on potatoes, sugar beets and
  peanuts, usually served on rice

ko·wee *kahn·*kah   *quwi kanka*
  fried guinea pig

Cuzco

chee·ree oo·choo   *chiri uchu*
a spicy dish of fried meat and hot peppers, especially popular during the Corpus Christi festival

lo·mo   *lomo* (Spanish)
fried beef prepared with onions, tomatoes, rice, potatoes, and a unique blend of seasonings

pah·ko·chah/   *paqucha/*
ahl·pah·kah ai·chah   *alpaka aycha*
alpaca meat

pe·pyahn de kui   *pepián de cuy* (Spanish)
fried rabbit or guinea pig served with rice and/or boiled potatoes

poo·chee·roo/teem·po   *puchiru/timpu*
soup of steak, lamb's head, bacon and raisins, often including cabbage, potatoes, chickpeas and rice

troo·chah   *trucha*
trout

Puno

kahn·kah·choo   *kankachu*
roast suckling pig, veal or lamb, prepared with hot peppers, ground spices, white wine, lemon, garlic, oil and pureed papaya

kah·rah·chee teem·poo   *karachi timpu*
thick fish stew made with *karachi*, kah·rah·chee (a fish from Lake Titicaca), *muña*, moo·nyah (an aromatic herb), *ch'uñu*, ch'oo·nyoo, garlic, onion and hot peppers

ke·so oo·mah·chah   *queso umacha*
stew made with hot peppers, farmers' cheese, diced onion, milk and eggs, served over boiled potatoes

AT THE MARKET

QHATUPI

Where can I find the ...?
mai·*pee*·tahkh ... kahn?

¿Maypitaq ... kan?

I want to buy some ...
...·tah rahn·*tee*·tah moo·*nah*·nee

...-ta rantiyta munani.

Meat & Poultry		Imaymana Aychakuna
beef	*wah*·kah *ai*·chah	*waka aycha*
chicken	*wahly*·pah *ai*·cha	*wallpa aycha*
dried meat/jerky	*ch'ahr*·kee	*ch'arki*
duck	*pah*·too *ai*·chah	*patu aycha*
eggs	*roon*·too	*runtu*
fat/grease	*wee*·rah	*wira*
goat	*kah*·brah *ai*·chah	*kabra aycha*
guinea pig	*ko*·wee *ai*·chah	*quwi aycha*
lamb	oo·*wee*·hah *ai*·chah	*uwiha aycha*
llama	*lyah*·mah *ai*·chah	*llama aycha*
meat	*ai*·chah	*aycha*
partridge	*lyoo*·t-hoo/	*lluthu/*
	yoo·too *ai*·chah	*yutu aycha*
pork	k-hoo·chee *ai*·chah	*khuchi aycha*
pork rind	k-hoo·chee *kah*·rahn	*khuchi qaran*
rabbit	*ko*·wee *ai*·chah	*quwi aycha*
ribs	*wahkh*·tah *ai*·chah	*waqta aycha*
tripe	*ch'oon*·chool	*ch'unchul*
turkey	*pah*·woo *ai*·chah	*pawu aycha*

Vegetables		Mikhuna Qurakuna
cabbage	*koo*·lees	*kulis*
capsicum	pee·*meen*·tah	*piminta*
carrot	sah·*noor*·yah	*sanurya*
corn kernels	wee·*nyah*·poo	*wiñapu*
corn (on the cob)	*chokh*·lyo ee·*lyah*·koo	*chuqllu illaku*
fava beans	*hah*·wahs	*hawas*
garlic	*ah*·hoos	*ahus*
hot pepper	ro·*ko*·to/oo·choo	*ruqutu/uchu*
lettuce	lee·*choo*·gah	*lichuga*

FOOD

onions (spring)	see·*wee*·lyah	*siwilla*
peas	ahl·*weer*·hahs	*alwirhas*
potato	*pah*·pah	*papa*
pumpkin	sah·*pah*·lyoo	*sapallu*
tomato	too·*mah*·tee	*tumati*

THE DIVINE POTATO

Andean legend relates that when the first Inca ruler *Manqu Khapaq* and his consort *Mama Uqllu* emerged from Lake Titicaca to found their empire, the first thing their god, *Wiraqucha*, wee·rah·ko·chah, did was to teach them to plant potato fields.

Andeans name new potato varieties in creative ways to reflect their shape, flavour and texture. The popular yellow potato is known as *runtu papa, roon*·too *pah*·pah: *runtu* is the Quechua word for 'egg', and this potato has similar qualities to a hard-boiled egg. Other names are equally evocative, such as the *yana ñawi, yah*·nah *nyah*·wee, or 'black-eyed potato', and the *q'uyu tawna, k'o*·yoo *tow*·nah, or 'purple walking cane'. There are nearly 4000 varieties of potato to be found in its place of origin, the Andes.

Pulses, Grains & Legumes   Ch'aki Rurukuna

barley	see·*wah*·rah	*siwara*
bread	*t'ahn*·tah	*t'anta*
cañihua	kah·*nyee*·wah	*qañiwa*
dried beans	poo·*roo*·too	*purutu*
flour	*hah*·k'o	*hak'u*
kiwicha	kee·*wee*·chah	*kiwicha*
maize (dried corn)	*sah*·rah	*sara*
quinoa	*kyoo*·nyah/*kyoo*·nah	*kiwña/kiwna*
red and black bean	wai·*roo*·roo	*wayruru*
rice	*ah*·roos	*arus*
turnip (wild)	*yoo*·yoo	*yuyu*
wheat	*tree*·yoo	*triyu*

Fruit | | Ruru

apple	mahn·*sah*·nah	*mansana*
avocado	*pahl*·tah	*palta*
banana	lah·*tah*·noos	*latanus*
fruit	*roo*·roo	*ruru*
medlar	nees·*pee*·roos/	*nispirus/*
(like crabapple)	wees·*wee*·roos	*wiswirus*
orange	lah·*rahn*·hah	*laranha*
peach	doo·*rahs*·noo	*durasnu*
sour cherry	kah·*poo*·lee/*reen*·dahs	*kapuli/rindas*
tumbo fruit	*teen*·teen	*tintin*

Dairy Products | Lichimanta Mikhuykuna

butter	mahn·tee·*kee*·lyah	*mantikilla*
cheese	*kee*·soo	*kisu*
milk	*lee*·chee	*lichi*

Spices & Condiments | Misk'ipakuna

chillies/hot pepper	*oo*·choo	*uchu*
cinnamon	kah·*nee*·lah	*kanila*
coriander *(cilantro)*	koo·*lahn*·troo	*kulantru*
garlic	*ah*·hoos	*ahus*
honey	lah·*chee*·wah/	*lachiwa/*
	ah·*nyah*·kah	*añaka*
huacatay	wah·*kah*·tai	*wakatay*
(aromatic herb)		
oil	ah·*see*·tee	*asiti*
parsley	pee·*ree*·heel	*pirihil*
pepper	pee·*meen*·tah	*piminta*
salt	*kah*·chee	*kachi*
sauce (of tomato	*oo*·choo *koo*·tah	*uchu kuta*
and hot pepper)		
sugar	mees·k'ee/ah·*soo*·kahr	*misk'i/asukar*

FOOD

DRINKS
Nonalcoholic

UKYANAKUNA
Ukyana

Every region has its typical fruit juices such as the *likwarus*, leek·*wah*·roos, 'fruit shakes', of Bolivia, widely available in cities. Soft drinks are rare but not impossible to find in rural areas, particularly during festivals and fairs. They're considered a great luxury for the highlanders, who usually drink herbal tea. One variety is *chicha* (*aqha/aha*, *ah*·k-hah/*ah*·hah, in Quechua) made from quinoa instead of corn.

chicha morada (made from purple corn)	*koo*·lyee *ah*·k-hah/*ah*·hah	*kulli aqha/aha*
coca leaf tea	*koo*·kah *mah*·tee	*kuka mati*
coffee	*kah*·fee	*kaphiy*
cold water	*chee*·ree oo·noo/*yah*·koo	*chiri unu/yaku*
corn tea (Bolivian)	*ah*·pee	*api*
(in Peru, *api* is purple cornstarch pudding)		
herbal tea	*ko*·rah oo·noo	*qura unu*
hot water	*k'o*·nyee oo·noo/*yah*·koo	*q'uñi unu/yaku*
juice	*hee*·lyee	*hilli*
lemonade	lee·moo·*nah*·rah	*limunara*
mineral water	woo·tee·*lyah*·pee oo·noo	*wutillapi unu*
soda/soft drink	*koo*·lah/gah·see·*yoo*·sah	*kula/gasiyusa*
tea ...	tee ...	*tiy* ...
with milk	lee·chee·*yokh*·tah	*lichiyuqta*
without milk	*mah*·nah lee·chee·*yokh*·tah	*mana lichiyuqta*
with sugar	mees·k'ee·*yokh*·tah; ah·soo·kahr·nee·*yokh*·tah	*misk'iyuqta asukarniyuqta*
without sugar	*mah*·nah mees·k'ee·*yokh*·tah; *mah*·nah ah·soo·kahr·nee·*yokh*·tah	*mana misk'iyuqta; mana asukarniyuqta*
toasted barley tea	see·*wah*·rah oo·noo	*siwara unu*
water	oo·noo/*yah*·koo	*unu/yaku*

FOOD

THE ANDEAN WONDER DRINK

The coca leaf has a long tradition of sacred and medicinal use in Andean cultures. It's most commonly chewed, or brewed as a tea, *kuka mati*, koo·kah mah·tee. The tea is prepared by pouring boiling water directly over the coca leaves, or by using coca tea bags which can be bought in any grocery store.

Coca's medicinal uses have been well documented. It's perhaps best known for its energising properties when one is hungry and tired, and for its ability to combat altitude sickness. Perhaps less well known by foreigners, but definitely appreciated by the locals, is its ability to aid digestion, cure diarrhoea and ease labour pains!

Alcoholic   Waqtu

Every region has its own special beers, wines and cocktails. Peru is known for *pisco*, pees·ko, a strong brandy distilled from grapes. *Chicha* or *aqha/aha*, ah·k-hah/ah·hah, is traditional corn beer, prepared and drunk throughout the Andean countries for centuries. *Singani*, seen·gah·nee, is a Bolivian drink made from a by-product of wine-making, mixed with lemon juice, lemon soda and ice.

beer	seer·wee·sah	sirwisa
brandy	trah·woo	trawu
chicha (maize beer)	ah·k-hah/ah·hah	aqha/aha
chicha bar	ah·k-hah wah·see	aqha wasi
singani	seen·gah·nee	singani

FOOD

QHALI KAY

Any health care in the high, remote Andes is likely to take place with a *hampiq*, hahm·pekh, 'healer' (or *curandero/a* (m/f) in Spanish), instead of a medical doctor. Healers use traditional folk medicine based on herbs, stones, potions and animal fats. Carry your own medicines or first aid kit with you when you're travelling, just to be on the safe side.

In metropolitan areas and populous regions, you'll always be able to find medical services. These places will operate in Spanish, as will the staff at the medical posts scattered few and far between in rural areas.

See Trekking, page 112, for advice on altitude sickness.

Is there a ...	*kahm*·choo ...	*¿Kanchu ...*
around here?	*kai*·pee?	*kaypi?*
chemist/ pharmacy	hahm·*pee*·yokh *wah*·see	*hampiyuq wasi*
dentist	*kee*·roo *see*·k'ekh	*kiru sikiq*
doctor	mee·*dee*·koo/*dook*·toor	*midiku/duktur*
healer	*hahm*·pekh	*hampiq*
hospital	hahm·*pee*·nah *wah*·see	*hampina wasi*

WITH THE HEALER   HAMPIQWAN

Could the healer come here?
  pahkh·tah hahm·*pekh*·kah   *¿Paqta hampiqqa*
  kai·mahn hah·moo·*rui*·mahn?   *kayman hamurquyman?*
I'm sick.
  on·ko·*shah*·neen   *Unqushanin.*
My friend is sick.
  rekh·see·nah·kokh·*mah*·see   *Riqsinakuqmasiy*
  on·*ko*·shahn   *unqushan.*
I have a toothache.
  kee·*rui*·mee nah·nah·*wah*·shahn *Kiruymi nanawashan.*

HEALTH

I've broken my tooth.

   kee·*rui*·mee p'ah·*kee*·roon   *Kiruymi p'akirqun.*

My mouth hurts.

   see·*mee*·mee nah·nah·*wah*·shahn   *Simiymi nanawashan.*

Ouch!   ah·chah·*kow!*   ¡*Achakáw!*

AILMENTS   UNQUYKUNA

I feel nauseous.

   mee·*lyah*·nah·yah·wah·   *Millanayawashanmi/*
   shahn·mee*l*

   wees·ch'oo·nah·yah·wah·   *Wisch'unayawashanmi.*
   shahn·mee

I feel under the weather.

   mah·nahn ah·*lyeen*·choo   *Manan allinchu*
   kah·*shah*·nee   *kashani.*

I feel weak.

   mah·nah kahly·pah·*yokh*·mee   *Mana kallpayuqmi*
   kah·*shah*·nee   *kashani.*

I'm ill.

   on·ko·*shah*·neen   *Unqushanin.*

THE HEALER MAY SAY ...

   ee·mah·nah·*soon*·keen?   ¿*Imanasunkin?*
     What's the matter?

   ee·mai·*lyai*·*kee*·pahs   ¿*Imallaykipas*
   nah·nah·soon·*kee*·choo?   *nanasunkichu?*
     Do you feel any pain?

   mai·peen nah·nah·   ¿*Maypin nanasunki?*
   soon·*kee?*
     Where does it hurt?

   e·*mai*·keen nah·nah·   ¿*Imaykin nanasunki?*
   soon·*kee?*
     What part of your body hurts?

THE HEALER MAY SAY ... (cont.)

HEALTH

roo·p-hai on·koi·wahn·choo kah·shahn·kee?	¿Ruphay unquywanchu kashanki?

Do you have a temperature?

hai·k'ah p'oon·chai·nyahn on·ko·shahn·kee?	¿Hayk'a p'unchayñan unqushanki?

How long have you been like this?

k'ee·koo·chee·koo· shahn·kee·choo?; yah·wahr·nee·kee·choo hah·moo·shan?	¿K'ikuchikushankichu?; ¿Yawarniykichu hamushan?

Are you menstruating?

week·sah·yokh·choo kah·shahn·kee?	¿Wiksayuqchu kashanki?

Are you pregnant?

kai (k'o·nyee) koo·kah mah·tee·tah ook·yah· kui·kui	Kay (q'uñi) kuka matita ukyakuykuy.

Drink this cup of (hot) coca leaf tea.

no·kahn hahm·pee·roo·sai·kee	Nuqan hampirqusayki.

I'll cure your illness.

ah·mah lyah·kee·kui·choo, koo·nah·chah·lyahn·mee ah·lyeen·yahn·kee	Ama llakikuychu, kunachallanmi allinyanki.

Don't worry, you'll get well soon.

ah·lyee·choo ... kai·pee	Allichu ... kaypi.	Please ... here.
see·ree·kui	sirikuy	lie down
tee·yah·kui	tiyakuy	sit down
poo·nyoo·kui	puñukuy	sleep
sah·mah·kui	samakuy	rest

It hurts here.
kai·pee nah·nah·wah·shahn *Kaypi nanawashan.*

I feel better/worse.
ah·lyeen·yah·shah·neen/ *Allinyashanin/*
seen·cheer·ko·shah·neen *Sinchirqushanin.*

I've been vomiting for (two days).
(ees·kai p'oon·chai·nyahn) *(Iskay p'unchayñan)*
week·ch'oo·pah·koo·nee *wikch'upakuni.*

I can't sleep.
mah·nahn poo·nyui·tah *Manan puñuyta*
ah·tee·nee·choo *atinichu.*

I burned myself.
roo·p·hah·chee·koo·roo·neen *Ruphachikurqunin.*

I've been bitten by a
dog/snake/insect.
ahl·ko/mah·ch'ahkh·wai/ *Alqu/Mach'aqway/*
koo·roo kah·nee·roo·wahn *Kuru kanirquwan.*

I've sprained my wrist/ankle.
mah·kee/chah·kee mo·koy·tahn *Maki/Chaki muquytan*
k'e·wee·koo·roo·nee *q'iwikurquni.*

I think I have worms.
week·sai·pee koo·roo·yokh·choos *Wiksaypi kuruyuqchus*
hee·nah kah·shah·nee *hina kashani.*

I have a rash.
k·hee·kee on·koy·wahn·mee *Khiki unquywanmi*
kah·shah·nee *kashani.*

I feel ...	...·*wahn*·mee	...-*wanmi*
	kah·*shah*·nee	*kashani.*
dizzy	*oo*·mah *moo*·yui	*uma muyuy*
shivery	k-hah·*tah*·tai	*khatatay*

HEALTH

I have (a/an) ...	...·*wahn*·mee	...-*wanmi*
	kah·*shah*·nee	*kashani.*
altitude sickness	soo·*roo*·chee	*suruchi*
bronchitis	*nee*·shoo oo·hoo	*nishu uhu*
chickenpox	sah·rahn·*pee*·yoon	*saranpiyun*
cold	*chee*·ree *on*·koy	*chiri unquy*
constipation	*ah*·kah *k'ees*·kee	*aka k'iski*
cough	*oo*·hoo	*uhu*
diarrhoea	*k'e*·chah *on*·koy	*q'icha unquy*
fever	*roo*·p-hai *on*·koy	*ruphay unquy*
fleas	*pee*·kee	*piki*
headache	*oo*·mah *nah*·nai	*uma nanay*
influenza	ch-*hoo*·lyee/	*chhulli*/
	hah·ch'ee	*hach'i*
lice	oo·sah·*koo*·nah	*usakuna*
lump	*k'om*·poo	*q'umpu*
malaria	*chookh*·choo *on*·koy	*chukchu unquy*
migraine	*nee*·shoo	*nishu*
	oo·mah *nah*·nai	*uma nanay*
rash	k-*hee*·keel/k-*heer*·kee	*khiki*/*khirki*
sore throat	*ton*·kor *nah*·nai	*tunqur nanay*
stomachache	*week*·sah *nah*·nai	*wiksa nanay*
sunburn	*roo*·p-hai	*ruphay*
toothache	*kee*·roo *nah*·nai	*kiru nanay*
urinary tract	*hees*·p'ai *p'ee*·tee/	*hisp'ay p'iti*/
infection	*on*·koy	*unquy*
wound	*k'ee*·ree	*k'iri*

HEALTH

WOMEN'S HEALTH

WARMIKUNAQ QHALI KAYNIN

Could I see a female healer?
*pahkh·tah warh·mee
hahm·pekh·wahn
hahm·pee·chee·kui·mahn?*

¿Paqta warmi
hampiqwan
hampichikuyman?

I'm pregnant.
week·sah·yokh·mee kah·nee

Wiksayuqmi kani.

I think I'm pregnant.
*week·sah·yoos·choos
hee·nah kah·shah·nee*

Wiksayuschus
hina kashani.

I haven't had my period
for ... weeks.
*...nyah yah·wahr·nee mah·nah
hah·moon·choo*

...-ña yawarniy mana
hamunchu.

SPECIAL HEALTH NEEDS

UNQUQKUNA QHALI KANANPAQ

I have ...   *...wahn·mee kah·shah·nee*   ...-wanmi kashani.
  anaemia   *ah·nee·mee·yah*   animiya
  asthma   *chah·k'ee oo·hoo*   chak'i uhu
  epilepsy   *wah·nyui on·koy*   wañuy unquy
  rheumatism   *too·lyoo nah·nai*   tullu nanay

I suffer from allergies.
ah·leer·hee·koon kah·nee

Alirhikun kani.

I have a weak heart.
mah·nahn ah·lyeen·choo son·koy

Manan allinchu sunquy.

I can't see very well.
*mah·nahn ah·lyeen·tah
ree·kui·tah ah·tee·nee·choo*

Manan allinta
rikuyta atinichu.

PARTS OF THE BODY   AYCHA KURKU KUNU

My ... hurts.
　...ee/·nee nah·nah·*wah*·shahn　　...-y/-niy nanawashan.

My ... is swollen.
　...ee/·nee poon·*kees*·kah　　...-y/-niy punkisqa
　kah·shahn　　kashan.

I can't move my ...
　mah·nahn ...*ee*·tah/·*nee*·tah　　Manan ...-yta/-niyta
　koo·yoo·*chee*·tah　　kuyuchiyta
　ah·tee·*nee*·choo　　atinichu.

HEALTH

FIX IT

Remember, when using the *-y/-niy* or *-yta/-niyta* suffixes
with words, choose the *-y* or *-yta* ending when the root
word ends in a vowel, and the *-niy* or *-niyta* ending
when it ends in a consonant.

---

ankle	*chah*·kee mo·*k-ho*·choo	chaki muquchu
arm	*mah*·keel/*mahr*·k'ah	maki/marq'a
back	*wah*·sah	wasa
bladder	*hees*·p'ai *poo*·roo	hisp'ay puru
bone	*too*·lyoo	tullu
bottom	*see*·kee	siki
breast	*nyoo*·nyoo	ñuñu
buttock	*see*·kee *pah*·pahn	siki papan
cheek	*k'ahkh*·lyah	k'aklla
chest	*k-hahs*·ko	qhasqu
ear	*reen*·reel/*neen*·ree	rinri/ninri
elbow	*k'oo*·*koo*·choo/	k'ukuchu/
	koo·choos	kuchus
eye	*nyah*·wee	ñawi
face	*oo*·yah	uya
finger	*roo*·k'ah/*ree*·roo	ruk'a/riru
foot	*chah*·kee	chaki
forehead	*mah*·t'ee	mat'i

HEALTH

hand	*mah*·kee	*maki*
head	*oo*·mah	*uma*
heart	*son*·ko	*sunqu*
hip	*see*·kee *pah*·tah	*siki pata*
jaw/chin	*k'ah*·kee	*k'aki*
kidney	*roo*·roon; *wah*·sah *roo*·roon	*rurun; wasa rurun*
knee	*mo*·ko/*kon*·kor	*muqu/qunqur*
leg	*chah*·kah	*chaka*
lips	*weer*·p'ah	*wirp'a*
liver	koo·*koo*·peen/ *k'eep*·chahn	*kukupin/ k'ipchan*
lungs	*sor*·k'ahn	*surq'an*
mouth	*see*·mee	*simi*
nail	*see*·lyoo	*sillu*
neck	*koon*·kah	*kunka*
nose	*sen*·kah	*sinqa*
penis	pee·*chee*·koo/*pees*·ko	*pichiku/pisqu*
rib	*wahkh*·tah	*waqta*
shoulder	*reek*·rah	*rikra*
skin	*kah*·rah	*qara*
spine	*wah*·sah *too*·lyoo	*wasa tullu*
stomach	*week*·sah	*wiksa*
teeth	*kee*·roo	*kiru*
tongue	*kah*·lyoo	*qallu*
throat	*ton*·kor/*ton*·ko·ree/ *k'ah*·sah	*tunqur/tunquri/ q'asa*
vagina	*rah*·k·hah	*rakha*
vein	*seer*·k'ah	*sirk'a*
waist	*we*·kow	*wiqaw*
wrist	*mah*·kee *mo*·ko	*maki muqu*

PACHAKUNAPAS RAYMIKUNAPAS
TIME, DATES & FESTIVALS

Time is flexibly defined in the Andes. While 'clock time' certainly exists, Andeans have set their schedules by the movement of the sun for centuries, and their ways of expressing the passing of time reflect this.

Despite the hard life of rural Andeans – or perhaps because of it – they find many reasons to celebrate. Weddings, baptisms, national and regional holidays, Carnival, Catholic holy days, patron saints' days and other traditional religious occasions are all reasons to take a break from work for a few hours or days.

TELLING THE TIME   URAMANTA RIMAY

Telling the time in Quechua is easy. To express the time in hours, you simply use the number for that hour, followed by *urasmi*, oo·*rahs*·mee:

It's (one) o'clock.
　(hokh) oo·*rahs*·mee   *(Huq) urasmi.*

To express the half hour, you add 'half', *kuskanniyuqmi*, koos·kahn·nee·*yokh*·mee, into the hour:

Half past one.
　hokh *oo*·rahs   *Huq uras kuskanniyuqmi.*
　koos·kahn·nee·*yokh*·mee

For any time between the hour and the half hour, you need to express how many minutes are added to the previous hour:

Quarter past one.
　hokh *oo*·rahs *choon*·kah   *Huq uras chunka*
　pees·*kah*·yokh   *pisqayuq*
　mee·noo·too·*yokh*·mee   *minutuyuqmi.*

TIME, DATES & FESTIVALS

What's the time?
ee·mah oo·*rahs*·mee *kah*·shahn?　¿*Ima urasmi kashan?*

It's twenty past three.
keen·sah oo·rahs *ees*·kai　*Kinsa uras iskay*
choon·kah pees·*kah*·yokh　*chunka pisqayuq*
mee·*noo*·too·*yokh*·mee　*minutuyuqmi.*

Likewise, time between the half hour and the hour to come is expressed by how many minutes are lacking until the next full hour:

It's quarter to four.
choon·kah pees·*kah*·yokh　*Chunka pisqayuq*
mee·*noo*·too p-*hahl*·tahn　*minutu phaltan*
tah·wah oo·*rahs*·pahkh　*tawa uraspaq.*

DAYS OF THE WEEK　P'UNCHAYKUNA

Monday	*loo*·nees	*lunis*
Tuesday	*mahr*·tees	*martis*
Wednesday	meer·*koo*·lees	*mirkulis*
Thursday	*hui*·wees	*huywis*
Friday	*weer*·nees	*wirnis*
Saturday	sah·*wah*·roo	*sawaru*
Sunday	doo·*meen*·goo	*dumingu*

MONTHS　KILLAKUNA

January	ee·*nee*·roo *kee*·lyah	*iniru killa*
February	p-hyoo·*ree*·roo *kee*·lyah	*phiwriru killa*
March	*mahr*·soo *kee*·lyah	*marsu killa*
April	*ow*·reel *kee*·lyah	*awril killa*
May	*mah*·yoo *kee*·lyah	*mayu killa*
June	hoo·*nee*·yoo *kee*·lyah	*huniyu killa*
July	hoo·*lee*·yoo *kee*·lyah	*huliyu killa*
August	ah·*woos*·too *kee*·lyah	*awustu killa*

September	see·*teem*·ree *kee*·lyah	*sitimri killa*
October	ook·*too*·ree *kee*·lyah	*uktuwri killa*
November	noo·*weem*·bree *kee*·lyah	*nuwimbri killa*
December	dee·*seem*·ree *kee*·lyah	*disimri killa*

SEASONS

MIT'AKUNA

autumn	*po*·koy *mee*·t'ah	*puquy mit'a*
spring	*chee*·row *mee*·t'ah	*chiraw mit'a*
summer	*roo*·p-hai *mee*·t'ah	*ruphay mit'a*
winter	*chee*·ree *mee*·t'ah	*chiri mit'a*
dry season	*ch'ah*·kee *mee*·t'ah	*ch'aki mit'a*
rainy season	*pah*·rah *mee*·t'ah	*para mit'a*

TIME, DATES & FESTIVALS

BY THE SUN ...

In areas where people don't own watches, they tell the time by the sun's movements.

inti siqay;   een·tee se·kai;
inti lluqsimuy   een·tee lyokh·see·mui
   dawn/sunrise ('the sun comes up')

inti llipipimuy   een·tee lyee·pee·pee·mui
   sunrise ('flickering sun')

inti t'iksuy;   een·tee t'eek·sui;
qhata inti   k-hah·tah een·tee
   late afternoon ('the sun leans'/'sloping sun')

inti haykuy   een·tee hai·kui
   sunset (sundown/'the sun goes down behind
   the horizon')

intiq lluqsinan   een·tekh llokh·see·nahn
   east ('where the sun comes up')

intiq chinkanan   een·tekh cheen·kah·nahn
   west ('where the sun disappears')

TIME, DATES & FESTIVALS

DATES

What's the date today?

ee·mah pah·*chah*·tahkh koo·nahn?

¿Ima pachataq kunan?

It's 18 October.

choon·kah poo·sahkh·*nee*·yokh
ook·*too*·ree kee·lyahn

Chunka pusaqniyuq
uktuwri killan.

Present

now	koo·nahn	kunan
today	koo·nahn p'oon·chai	kunan p'unchay
tonight	ch'ee·*see*·mahn	ch'isiman
this ...	koo·nahn ...	kunan ...
morning	too·tah·*mahn*·tahn	tutamantan
afternoon	een·tee teek·*sui*·pee;	inti t'iksuypi;
	tai·*ree*·mahn	tayriman
night	too·tah	tuta
week	see·*mah*·nah	simana
month	kee·lyah	killa
year	wah·tah	wata

PACHAKUNA

Kunan Pacha

Past

yesterday	kai·nah p'oon·chai	qayna p'unchay
day before	kai·*neem*·pah	qaynimpa
yesterday	p'oon·chai	p'unchay
yesterday ...	kai·nah ...	qayna ...
morning	too·tah·*mahn*·tahn	tutamantan
afternoon	een·tee	inti
evening	t'eek·*sui*·pee/ch'ee·see	t'iksuypi/ch'isi
last ...	kai·nah ...	qayna ...
night	too·tah	tuta
week	see·*mah*·nah	simana
month	kee·lyah	killa
year	wah·tah	wata
since (May)	(mah·yoo kee·lyah)·	(mayu killa)-
	mahn·tah	manta

Qayna Pacha

TIME, DATES & FESTIVALS

Future / Hawa Pacha

tomorrow ...	pah·*kah*·reen ...	paqarin ...
morning	too·tah·*mahn*·tahn	tutamantan
afternoon	een·tee teek·*sui*·pee;	inti t'iksuypi;
	tai·*ree*·mahn	tayriman
evening	*ch'ee*·see	ch'isi
day after tomorrow	*meen*·ch-hah	minchha
next ...	*k'ah*·yah/*hah*·wah ...	q'aya/hawa ...
week	see·*mah*·nah	simana
month	*kee*·lyah	killa
year	*wah*·tah	wata

in (five) minutes
(*pees*·kah) mee·noo·too·*mahn*·tah   (pisqa) minutumanta
until (June)
(hoo·*nee*·yoo kee·lyah)·*kah*·mah   (huniyu killa)-kama

DURING THE DAY / P'UNCHAYPI

afternoon	een·tee *t'eek*·sui; *tai*·ree	inti t'iksuy; tayri
dawn	een·tee se·kai/*lyokh*·see	inti siqay/lluqsiy
day	*p'oon*·chai/*p'oon*·chow	p'unchay/p'unchaw
early	too·tah·lyah·*mahn*·tah	tutallamanta
evening	*ch'ee*·seen	ch'isin
lunchtime	mee·k-hui *oo*·rah	mikhuy ura
midday	chow·pee *p'oon*·chai	chawpi p'unchay
midnight	chow·pee *too*·tah	chawpi tuta
morning	too·tah·*mahn*·tahn	tutamantan
night	*too*·tah	tuta
noon	chow·pee *p'oon*·chai	chawpi p'unchay

FESTIVALS & NATIONAL HOLIDAYS   RAYMIKUNAPAS HATUN P'UNCHAYKUNAPAS

The Andean countries are predominantly Catholic, and numerous holy days and ancient traditions fill the celebration calendar. Any religious event is also a social event, a reason to gather and celebrate.

Inti Raymi   *een·tee rai·mee*

The 'Festival of the Sun' honours the sun god, the highest of the Andean deities, and is a week-long celebration held during the winter solstice. The high point of the festival occurs in Sacsayhuamán, just outside of Cuzco. 24 June is the day of *Inti Raymi*, which marks the beginning of the sun's New Year. It was banned for centuries by the Catholic church, but continued to be held in secret.

Mamacha Kandilarya   mah·*mah*·chah
                                        kahn·dee·*lahr*·yah
The Festival of the Virgin of the Candelaria. She is the patron
saint of both Bolivia and Peru and is known throughout South
America as a worker of great miracles. Festivities in her honour
– parades, music, dancing, food and drink, and an interesting
mix of Andean and Catholic religious rituals – begin a week
prior to 2 February. The colour and incomparable majesty of
these events is a prelude to Carnival.

Karnawal   kahr·*nah*·wahl
Carnival is celebrated throughout South America, but takes
on a uniquely Andean flavour in Bolivia, Peru and Ecuador,
where each region has its own special traditions. The week-long
celebrations take place the week before Ash Wednesday on the
Catholic calendar. Everyone lives it up before the fasting and
sacrifice of Lent.

Día de Todos los Santos   dee·ah de *to*·dos los *sahn*·tos
Día de los Muertos   dee·ah de los *mwer*·tos
All Saints' Day on 1 November and All Souls' Day, the
next day, are more than a simple observance honouring the
saints and departed family members – they have become
enmeshed with Andean beliefs and practices for honouring
the dead. After attending Mass, community members prepare a
feast, often served in the local cemetery so that departed family
members can participate. There are always some favourite dishes
– often lavishly decorated – of those who have passed away.

Nawida P'unchay   nah·*wee*·dah *p'oon*·chai
Midnight Mass and street celebrations with music, dancing,
food and drinks on Christmas Eve and Christmas Day are
common. You'll see the nativity scene everywhere in homes and
churches. In less Christian areas, Christmas may be celebrated
as a harvest festival.

Año Nuevo   *ah·nyo nwe·vo*
New Year's Eve and New Year's Day are included in the general
Christmas festivities. Regional traditions involve processions,
gatherings and public dancing where everyone joins in. In some
parts of Bolivia, the Christmas season celebrations last until the
end of January.

Día de los Reyes Magos   *dee·ah de los re·yes mah·gos*
Epiphany, or the Feast of the Three Kings, on 6 January,
marks the end of the Christmas season. It's the day children
traditionally receive their Christmas gifts.

Fiestas Patrias   *fyes·tahs pah·tryahs*
Every Latin American country celebrates the day it
achieved independence from Spain. It's a time of parties
and demonstrations of patriotism, people wave flags and
sing national anthems during the colourful parades. Peru's
Independence Day is 28 July, Bolivia's 6 August and
Ecuador's 10 August.

Día del Santo Patrón   *dee·ah del sahn·to pah·tron*
National, regional and local patron saints' days vary according
to the saint being honoured. The festivities may be one to
several days in length, and generally include music and dancing,
as well as special Masses and services. They are as much a social
event and party as a dedicated religious observance – saints' day
celebrations are a treat not to be missed.

Aniversario de Fundación   *ah·nee·ver·sah·ryo de*
                                                        foon·dah·syon
Many cities, towns and villages celebrate the anniversary of their
founding. Since these are secular celebrations, there may or may
not be a special Mass offered, but there'll always be typical
Andean festivities.

CHRISTENINGS & WEDDINGS

ULIYAYKUNAPAS KASARAKUYKUNAPAS

Given the wide variety of traditions, weddings can be performed and celebrated in very different ways. Christenings, on the other hand, are fairly uniform due to the influence of Catholicism. They're an all-day affair, accompanied by a feast put on by the godparents. As with other celebrations, there is much singing and dancing, eating and drinking.

Congratulations!
  koo·see·*koos*·pah
  kow·sah·koon·*kee*·chees!

¡Kusikuspa
kawsakunkichis!

To the bride and groom!
  kah·sah·rahkh·*koo*·nah
  how·*kah*·lyah kow·sah·*choon*·koo!

¡Kasaraqkuna
hawkalla kawsachunku!

baptism	oo·lee·yoo/wow·*tee*·soo	*uliyu/wawtisu*
to baptise/ christen	oo·*lee*·yai/oo·*noo*·chai/ wow·*tee*·sai	*uliyay/unuchay/ wawtisay*
to celebrate	k'o·choo·*ree*·chee/ fees·*tee*·hai	*q'uchurichiy/ phistihay*
to celebrate (a birthday)	fees·*tah*·kui	*phistakuy*
festival	*rai*·mee	*raymi*
gift	ree·koo·*chee*·kui	*rikuchikuy*
goddaughter	ai·*hah*·rah	*ayhara*
godfather	pah·*ree*·noo	*parinu*
godmother	mah·*ree*·nah	*marina*
godparent	mahr·*k'ah*·ke	*marq'aqi*
godson	ai·*hah*·roo	*ayharu*
holiday	*hah*·toon fees·tah	*hatun phista*
party	*fees*·tah	*phista*
wedding	kahk·sah·*rah*·kui	*kasarakuy*
wedding present	kah·sah·rahkh·koo·*nah*·pahkh ree·koo·*chee*·kui	*kasaraqkunapaq rikuchikuy*

TIME, DATES & FESTIVALS

TIME, DATES & FESTIVALS

TOASTS & CONDOLENCES

ANQUSAYKUNAPAS LLAKIPAYKUNAPAS

Bon appetit!
  mees·k'ee·lyah·*tah*·nyah
  mee·*k-hoo*·kui!

¡Misk'illataña mikhukuy!

Bon voyage!
  ah·lyeen·*lyah*·nyah poo·*ree*·kui!

¡Allinllaña purikuy!

Cheers!
  ook·yai·*koo*·soon!

¡Ukyaykusun!

Good luck!
  ah·lyeen sah·*mee*·yokh kai!

¡Allin samiyuq kay!

Hope it goes well!
  ee·*chah*·pahs roo·wahs·*kai*·kee
  ah·lyeen *kahm*·mahn!

¡Ichapas ruwasqayki allin kanman!

What bad luck!
  ee·mah *k-hen*·chah!

¡Ima qhincha!

Never mind!
  mah·nah ee·mah·nahn·*pahs*·choo!

¡Mana imananpaschu!

Get well soon!
  oos·k·*hai*·lyah ah·lyeen·*yah*·yai!

¡Usqhaylla allinyayay!

I'm very sorry.
  ahn·*chah*·tahn lyah·kee·*pai*·kee

Anchatan llakipayki.

My deepest sympathy.
  seen·*chee*·tahn lyah·kee·*pai*·kee

Sinchitan llakipayki.

YUPAKUNAPAS HAYK'AKUNAPAS

NUMBERS & AMOUNTS

The numbers from zero to 10 each have their own name. These 'basic' numbers are also used to form the numbers from 11 to 19, which are expressed as '10 with one' through to '10 with nine'. The suffix *-yuq*, *-yokh*, 'with', is added to the end of units, not to the tens. Forming the tens is easy too: 20 is 'two tens', 30 is 'three tens', and so on. Remember that when a number ends in a consonant, the suffix *-ni* needs to be added before the suffix *-yuq*. For example, the number 11 is formed by joining *huq* for 'one' and *chunka* for '10' – *chunka huqniyuq*, *choon·kah hokh·nee·yokh*.

To count from 100 onwards, you use the same system as for the numbers one to 100. Thus the number 2002 would be *iskay waranqa iskayniyuq*, *ees·*kai wah·*rahn·*kah ees·kai·*nee·*yokh (lit: two thousand two-with).

CARDINAL NUMBERS   IMAKAQ YUPAKUNA

0	*ch'oo·*sahkh	*ch'usaq*
1	hokh	*huq*
2	*ees·*kai	*iskay*
3	*keen·*sah	*kinsa*
4	*tah·*wah	*tawa*
5	*pees·*kah	*pisqa*
6	*sokh·*tah	*suqta*
7	*kahn·*chees	*qanchis*
8	*poo·*sakh	*pusaq*
9	*ees·*kon	*isqun*
10	*choon·*kah	*chunka*
11	*choon·*kah hokh·*nee·*yokh	*chunka huqniyuq*
12	*choon·*kah ees·kai·*nee·*yokh	*chunka iskayniyuq*

13	*choon*·kah keen·*sah*·yokh	chunka kinsayuq
14	*choon*·kah tah·*wah*·yokh	chunka tawayuq
15	*choon*·kah pees·*kah*·yokh	chunka pisqayuq
16	*choon*·kah sokh·*tah*·yokh	chunka suqtayuq
17	*choon*·kah kahn·chees·*nee*·yokh	chunka qanchisniyuq
18	*choon*·kah poo·sahkh·*nee*·yokh	chunka pusaqniyuq
19	*choon*·kah ees·kon·*nee*·yokh	chunka isqunniyuq
20	*ees*·kay *choon*·kah	iskay chunka
21	*ees*·kay *choon*·kah hokh·*nee*·yokh	iskay chunka huqniyuq
22	*ees*·kay *choon*·kah ees·kai·*nee*·yokh	iskay chunka iskayniyuq
30	*keen*·sah *choon*·kah	kinsa chunka
40	*tah*·wah *choon*·kah	tawa chunka
50	*pees*·kah *choon*·kah	pisqa chunka
60	*sokh*·tah *choon*·kah	suqta chunka
70	*kahn*·chees *choon*·kah	qanchis chunka
80	*poo*·sakh *choon*·kah	pusaq chunka
90	*ees*·kon *choon*·kah	isqun chunka
100	*pah*·chahkh	pachak
1000	wah·*rahn*·kah	waranqa
1,000,000	*hoo*·noo	hunu

ORDINAL NUMBERS   ÑIQI YUPAKUNA

To form ordinal numbers, add either *ñiqin*, nye·ken, meaning 'order' or *kaq*, kahkh, meaning 'that which is' to the cardinal number; these endings can be used interchangeably. Note that '1st' is an exception:

1st	*nyow*·pahkh kahkh	ñawpaq kaq
2nd	*ees*·kai kahkh	iskay kaq
3rd	*keen*·sah kahkh	kinsa kaq

FRACTIONS

1/2	*ees*·kai *tah*·k'ah	*iskay taq'a*
1/3	*keen*·sah *tah*·k'ah	*kinsa taq'a*
1/4	*tah*·wah *tah*·k'ah	*tawa taq'a*
3/4	*keen*·sah *tah*·wah *tah*·k'ah	*kinsa tawa taq'a*

P'AKIKUNA

AMOUNTS

HAYK'AKAKUNA

How many/much?	*hai*·k'ah?	*¿Hayk'a?*
I need ...	...tah moo·*mah*·nee	*...ta munani.*
all	*lyah*·pahn/*too*·kui/lyoo	*llapan/tukuy/lliw*
(just) a little	*ahs*·lyah/*pee*·see/ chee·*kah*·lyah	*aslla/pisi/ chikalla*
some/a few	wah·*kee*·lyahn/ *pee*·see/*ahs*·lyah	*wakillan/ pisi/aslla*
enough	chai·*lyah*	*chaylla*
few	*ahs*·lyah; ahs pee·*see*·lyah; chee·kahn; *toom*·pah	*aslla; as pisilla; chikan; tumpa*
less	*pee*·see	*pisi*
many/much/ a lot	*ahs*·k·hah; *yoo*·pah; mai *chee*·kahn; mai·*too*·kui	*askha; yupa; may chikan; maytukuy*
more	ahs·*tah*·wahn	*astawan*
none/nothing	*mah*·nah ee·*mah*·pahs	*mana imapas*
once	hokh *koot*·ee	*huq kuti*
plenty	*lyah*·sahkh	*llasaq*
some	*toom*·pah/*ahs*·lyah	*tumpa/aslla*
too many/much	*ahs*·k·hah/*seen*·chee/ mai·*too*·kui/*lyah*·sahkh	*askha/sinchi/ maytukuy/llasaq*

NUMBERS & AMOUNTS

JUST GIVE ME ...

a bottle	hokh woo·*tee*·lyah	*huq wutilla*
a dozen	*choon*·kah	*chunka*
	ees·kai·nee·yokh·*neen*·teen;	*iskayniyuq-nintin;*
	hokh doo·*see*·nah	*huq dusina*
half a kilo	*meed*·yoo *kee*·loo	*midyu kilu*
half a dozen	*meed*·yah doo·*see*·nah	*midya dusina*
a kilo	wah·*rahn*·kah *ahkh*·noo	*waranqa-aqnu*
a hand full	hahp-h·t'ai	*hapht'ay*
two handfuls	*pot*·koi	*putquy*
100 grams	*pah*·chahkh-*ahkh*·noo	*pachak-aqnu*
a packet	hokh pah·*kee*·tee	*huq pakiti*
a pair	ees·kai·*neen*·teen	*iskaynintin*
a piece	*ahkh*·noo	*aqnu*
a pile	ko·too/*row*·k-hah/ *moon*·toon/*tow*·kah	*qutu/rawkha/ muntun/tawqa*

In rural and remote areas, Quechua could be vital.

Fire!	*nee*·nah roo-*p-hah*·shahn!	¡Nina ruphashan!
Go away!	*ree*·pui!;	¡Ripuy!;
	lyokh·see kai·*mahn*·tah!	¡Lluqsiy kaymanta!
Help!	yah·nah·*pah*·wai!	¡Yanapaway!
Stop!	*sah*·yai!	¡Sayay!
Thief!	*soo*·wah!	¡Suwa!
Watch out!	pahkh·*tah*·tahkh!/	¡Paqtataq!/
	ah·chah·*chow*!	¡Achacháw!

It's an emergency.
    seen·chee os·k·hai·*pahkh*·mee;   *Sinchi usqhaypaqmi;*
    nee·shoo pree·see·*sahkh*·mee   *Nishu prisisaqmi.*

Could you help us please?
    ah·*lyee*·choo yah·nah·pah-   *¿Allichu yanapa-*
    wahn·kee·koo·*mahn*·choo?   *wankikumanchu?*

Could I please use the telephone?
    ah·*lyee*·choo tee·lee·foo·*noo*·wahn   *¿Allichu tiliphunuwan*
    ree·mai·kui·*mahn*·choo?   *rimaykuymanchu?*

I'm lost.
    cheen·*kahs*·kahn kah·*shah*·nee;   *Chinkasqan kashani;*
    cheen·*kahs*·kahn poo·ree·*shah*·nee   *Chinkasqan purishani.*

Where are the toilets?
    mai·*pee*·tahkh hees·p'ah·*koo*·nah   *¿Maypitaq hisp'akuna*
    kah·shahn?; mai·*pee*·tahkh   *kashan?; ¿Maypitaq*
    hees·p'ah·*kui*·mahn?   *hisp'akuyman?*

Call a doctor/healer!
    mee·dee·*koo*·tah/hahm·*pekh*·tah   *!Midikuta/Hampiqta*
    wahkh·*yah*·mui!   *waqyamuy!*

I'm ill.
    on·*kos*·kahn kah·*shah*·nee   *Unqusqan kashani.*

My friend is ill.
    rekh·see·nah·kokh·mah·*see*·mee   *Riqsinakuqmasiymi*
    on·*ko*·shahn   *unqushan.*

POLICE

WARDIYA

Call the police!
wahr·dee·*yah*·tah wahkh·*yah*·mui!   ¡Wardiyata waqyamuy!

Where's the police station?
mai·*pee*·tahkh koo·mee·sah·*ree*·yah   ¿Maypitaq kumisariya
kah·shahn?   kashan?

I've been robbed.
soo·wah·chee·koo·*roo*·neen   Suwachikurqunin.

My ... was/	...*ee*·tahn *soo*·wah	...-ytan suwa
were stolen.	ah·*pah*·koon	apakun.
I've lost	...*ee*·tahn	...-ytan
my ...	cheen·kah·chee·*roo*·nee	chinkachirquni.
backpack	*ke*·pee	qipi
bags	mah·lee·tai·koo·*nah*·tahn	malitaykunatan
handbag	wah·*yah*·kah/*ch'oos*·pah	wayaqa/ch'uspa
money	*kol*·ke	qulqi
papers	doo·koo·meen·tui·koo·*nah*·tahn	dukumintuy-kunatan
wallet	*kol*·ke choo·*rah*·nah/wee·lyee·*tee*·rah	qulqi churana/willitira
(not) guilty	(*mah*·nah) hoo·*chah*·yokh	(mana) huchayuq
police officer	*tai*·tah wahr·*dee*·yah	tayta wardiya
police station	koo·mee·sah·*ree*·yah	kumisariya
rape	ahl·*ko*·chai	alquchay
robbery/theft	soo·*wah*·kui	suwakuy

A

English	Pronunciation	Quechua
to be able	*ah·tee*	*atiy*
above	hah·*wahn*·pee	*hawanpi*
abroad	*kah·*roo lyahkh·tah	*karu llaqta*
to accept	*ui*·nee	*uyniy*
accident	ahkh·see·*deen*·tee	*aksidinti*
accommodation	kor·pah·*chah*·nah	*qurpachana*
ache	*nah*·nai	*nanay*
across (from)	cheem·*pah*·pee	*chimpapi*
adult	*wee*·nyai hoon·*t'ahs*·kah •	*wiñay hunt'asqa* •
	kaly·*pah*·yokh	*kallpayuq*
advice	*yoo*·yai koy	*yuyay quy*
to advise (inform)	*wee*·lyai	*willay*
to advise (counsel)	yoo·*yai*·chai	*yuyaychay*
aeroplane	ah·*wee*·yoon	*awiyun*
to be afraid	mahn·*chah*·kui	*manchakuy*
afterwards	chai·mahn·*tah*·kah	*chaymantaqa*
again	hokh·*mahn*·tah	*huqmanta*
against	*koon*·trah	*kuntra*
ago (a while ago)	hokh rah·*too*·nyah	*huq ratuña*
to agree to	oo·*yah*·kui	*uyakuy*
ahead	*nyow*·pahkh	*ñawpaq*
air	*wai*·rah	*wayra*
alcohol	*wahkh*·too	*waqtu*
all	*lyah*·pah	*llapa*
to allow	sah·*ke*·lyai	*saqillay*
almost	*yah*·kah	*yaqa*
alone	*sah*·pah	*sapa*
already	·nyah	*-ña*
also (interchangeable)	·pees • ·pahs	*-pis* • *-pas*
although	*chai*·pahs	*chaypas*
always	*pah*·sahkh koo·*tee*·lyah	*pasaq kutilla*
among	oo·*k·hoo*·pee	*ukhupi*
ancient	*nyow*·pah	*ñawpa*
angry	*p·hee*·nyah	*phiña*
another	hokh	*huq*
to answer	koo·*tee*·chee	*kutichiy*
anything	ee·mah·*lyah*·pahs	*imallapas*
to argue	choo·rah·*nah*·kui	*churanakuy*
to arrive	*chai*·yai	*chayay*
to ask (a question)	*tah*·pui	*tapuy*
to ask (for something)	mah·*nyah*·kui	*mañakuy*
awful	*mah*·p'ah	*map'a*

B

English	Pronunciation	Quechua
baby (human)	wah·wah	wawa
baby (animal)	oo·nyah	uña
babysitter	wah·wah k-hah·wahkh	wawa qhawaq
backpack	k'ee·pee	q'ipi
bad	mah·nah ah·lyeen	mana allin
bag (large)	wah·yah·kah	wayaqa
bag (small)	ch'oos·pah	ch'uspa
baggage	mah·lee·tah	malita
ball	pee·loo·tah	piluta
band (music)	koo·see·tui	kusituy
bank (shore)	kahn·too	kantu
baptism	oo·lee·yai	uliyay
to barter	ch-hah·lai	chhalay
basket	kah·nahs·tah	kanasta
to bathe	ahr·mah·kui	armakuy
bathroom	bah·nyoo	bañu
to be	kai	kay
to bear (put up with)	ah·tee·pai	atipay
bear (animal)	oo·koo·koo	ukuku
beautiful	soo·mahkh	sumaq
bed	poo·nyoo·nah	puñuna
bedroom	poo·nyoo·nah kwahr·too	puñuna kwartu
before (time)	nyow·pahkh·tah	ñawpaqta
to begin	kah·lyah·ree	qallariy
behind	k-he·pah	qhipa
to believe (religious)	ee·nee • ee·nyee	iniy • iñiy
below	oo·rai	uray
beside	wahkh·tahn·pee	waqtanpi
besides (furthermore)	hee·nahs·pah	hinaspa
better	ahs·wahn ah·lyeen	aswan allin
bicycle	wee·see·kee·lee·tah	wisiklita
big	hah·toon	hatun
bigger	ahs·wahn hah·toon	aswan hatun
birthday	wah·tah hoon·t'ai	wata hunt'ay
to bite (any creature)	kah·nee	kaniy
to bite (of an insect)	k'oo·tui	k'utuy
to bite (of a dog; chew off something)	k-hah·chui	khachuy
blanket	kah·tah • choo·see	qata • chusi
to bleed	yah·wahr·chai	yawarchay
blind (adj)	nyow·sah	ñawsa
blood	yah·wahr	yawar
to bloom/blossom	see·sai	sisay
blue (of eyes only)	k-ho·see	qhusi

boat	*wahm*·poo	wampu
body	*ai*·chah *koor*·koo	aycha kurku
book	*lyoo*·roo	liwru
border	*sai*·wah	saywa
bored/boring	ah·*mees*·kah	amisqa
to borrow	mah·*nui*·pee *mah*·nyai	manuypi mañay
both	ees·*kai*·neen	iskaynin
to bother	*ch'ekh*·mee	ch'iqmiy
bottle	woo·*tee*·lyah	wutilla
bottle opener	woo·*tee*·lyah kee·*chah*·nah	wutilla kichana
bottom (body)	*see*·kee	siki
boy	*er*·ke	irqi
boyfriend	*yah*·nah	yana
bread	*t'ahn*·tah	t'anta
to break	*p'ah*·kee	p'akiy
breakfast	too·tah·*mahn*·tah mee·*k·hoo*·nah	tutamanta mikhuna
breasts	*nyoo*·nyoo	ñuñu
to breathe	sah·*mah*·ree	samariy
bridge	*chah*·kah	chaka
to bring	ah·*pah*·mui	apamuy
broken	p'ah·*kees*·kah	p'akisqa
to build	per·*kah*·chai	pirqachay
building	*hah*·toon wah·see	hatun wasi
bull	*too*·roo	turu
bullfighting	*too*·roo pookh·*lyai*	turu pukllay
burn	*roo*·p·hai	ruphay
to burn	roo·*p·hah*·chee	ruphachiy
busy (employed)	roo·wah·*nah*·yokh	ruwanayuq
busy (no free time)	*mah*·nah kah·sekh	mana qasiq
but	ee·*chah*·kah	ichaqa
butter	mahn·tee·*kee*·lyah	mantikilla
to buy	*rahn*·tee	rantiy

C

cabbage	*koo*·lees	kulis
calf	*oo*·nyah	uña
to call (by shouting)	*wahkh*·yai	waqyay
to call (to name)	soo·*tee*·chai	sutichay
can (to be able)	*ah*·tee	atiy
can (of food)	*lah*·tah	lata
can opener	*lah*·tah kee·*chah*·nah	lata kichana
candles	bee·*lah*·koo·nah	bilakuna
capital city	*oo*·mah *lyahkh*·tah	uma llaqta

car	kah·rroo	karru
care	k-hah·wai	qhaway
to carry (on the back)	k'e·pee	q'ipiy
cassette	kah·see·tee	kasiti
Catholic	kah·too·lee·koo	katuliku
cave	mah·ch'ai	mach'ay
to celebrate	k'oo·choo·kui	q'uchukuy
cemetery	ah·yah p'ahm·pah·nah	aya p'ampana
ceramic	k'ahkh·rah	k'akra
chair	tee·yah·nah	tiyana
to change (become different)	hokh·nee·rah·yai	huqnirayay
to change (exchange)	kahm·bee·yai	kambiyay
to cheat	k'o·tui	q'utuy
cheese	kee·soo	kisu
chest	k-hahs·ko	qhasqu
chewing gum	cheek·lee	chikli
chicha (maize beer)	ah·hah • ah·k-hah	aha • aqha
chicha bar	ah·hah·wah·see	ahawasi
chicken	wahly·pah	wallpa
child	wah·wah	wawa
chocolate	mees·k'ee • choo·koo·lah·tee	misk'i • chukulati
to choose	ahkh·lyai	akllay
church	een·lee·sah	inlisa
cigarette	see·yah·roo	siyaru
cinema	see·nee	sini
city	lyahkh·tah	llaqta
clean (of objects)	lui·loo	luylu
clean (of water)	ch'oo·yah	ch'uya
to clean	pee·chai	pichay
cliff	kah·kah	qaqa
to climb	wee·chai	wichay
clock	ree·lookh	riluh
to close	wees·k'ai	wisq'ay
close (near)	sees·pah	sispa
clothes	p'ah·chah	p'acha
coat	sah·koo	saku
coast	koos·tah	kusta
to collect	pah·lyai	pallay
colour	lyeem·pee	llimpi
to come	hah·mui	hamuy
comedian	ah·see·chee·kokh	asichikuq
to comfort	kahly·pah·chah·ree	kallpachariy
to communicate	wee·lyai	willay
community	ai·lyoo	ayllu

English	Pronunciation	Quechua
community leader	hah·mow·t'ah	hamawt'a
constipation	k'ees·kee	k'iski
to cook	wai·k'ui	wayk'uy
corn	sah·rah	sara
corn on the cob	chokh·lyo	chuqllu
corner (outside)	k'oo·choo	k'uchu
corner (inside)	hoo·k'ee	huk'i
to cost	kwees·tai	kwistay
country (nation)	lyahkh·tah	llaqta
countryside	pahm·pah	pampa
cough	ch'oo·hoo • oo·hoo	ch'uhu • uhu
to cough	oo·hui	uhuy
to count	yoo·pai	yupay
courtyard	kahn·chah	kancha
cow	wah·kah	waka
crazy	wah·k'ah	waq'a
to cross	cheem·pai	chimpay
cross (angry)	p-hee·nyahs·kah	phiñasqa
crowd	tahn·tah	tanta
to cry	wah·kai	waqay
cup	sui·k'oo	suyk'u
cup (Incas ceremonial)	ke·roo	qiru
to cure	hahm·pee	hampiy
to cut	koo·chui	kuchuy

D

English	Pronunciation	Quechua
daily	sah·pah p'oon·chai	sapa p'unchay
damp	ho·k'o	huq'u
dance	too·sui	tusuy
to dance	too·sui	tusuy
danger	mahn·chai	manchay
dark (night)	too·tah	tuta
to get dark	too·tah·yai	tutayay
date of birth	wah·tah·hoon·t'ai	wata hunt'ay
dawn	ee·lyah·ree • rahn·k-hee	illariy • rankhi
day	p'oon·chai	p'unchay
dead	wah·nyoos·kah	wañusqa
deaf	oo·pah	upa
to decide	kah·mah·ree·kui	kamarikuy
deep	oo·k-hoo	ukhu
delay	oo·nai	unay
to delay	oo·nai	unay
delicious	mees·k'ee	misk'i
dentist	kee·roo see·k'ekh	kiru sik'iq
to deny	mah·nahn nee	manan niy

to depart	*lyokh·see*	*lluqsiy*
descendent	*k-he·pah wee·nyai*	*qhipa wiñay*
desert	*ah·ko pahm·pah*	*aqu pampa*
to detour	*wahkh·lyee*	*waqlliy*
diarrhoea	*k'e·chah*	*q'icha*
to have diarrhoea	*k'e·chai*	*q'ichay*
to die	*wah·nyui*	*wañuy*
different	*hokh·nee·rahkh*	*huqniraq*
difficult	*sah·sah*	*sasa*
to direct	*yah·chah·chee*	*yachachiy*
dirty	*k-hahr·kah*	*kharka*
to disturb	*tah·koo·ree*	*takuriy*
dizzy	*oo·mah moo·yoos·kah*	*uma muyusqa*
to do/make	*roo·wai*	*ruway*
doctor	*dookh·toor*	*duktur*
done	*roo·wahs·kah*	*ruwasqa*
door	*poon·koo*	*punku*
to draw	*se·k'en·chai*	*siq'inchay*
dream/to dream	*mos·k-hoy*	*musqhuy*
dress	*p'ah·chah*	*p'acha*
to dress (oneself)	*p'ah·chah·lyee·kui*	*p'achallikuy*
to dress (someone else)	*p'ah·chah·lyee·chee*	*p'achallichiy*
drink/to drink	*ookh·yai*	*ukyay*
drug	*hahm·pee*	*hampi*
drugstore	*hahm·pee·yokh wah·see*	*hampiyuq wasi*
drum (small)	*teen·yah*	*tinya*
drum (large)	*wahn·kahr*	*wankar*
drunk	*mah·chahkh*	*machaq*
to get drunk	*mah·chai*	*machay*
dry	*ch'ah·kee*	*ch'aki*

E

each	*sah·pah*	*sapa*
early morning	*too·tah·lyah·mahn·tah*	*tutallamanta*
early afternoon	*ah·lyeen·pee·rahkh*	*allinpiraq*
to earn (money)	*tah·ree*	*tariy*
earth (soil)	*aly·pah*	*allpa*
the Earth	*kay pah·chah*	*kay pacha*
earth goddess (Mother Earth)	*pah·chah·mah·mah*	*Pachamama*
earthquake	*pah·chah koo·yui*	*pacha kuyuy*
east	*een·tee lyokh·see·mui*	*inti lluqsimuy*
easy	*fah·seel*	*phasil*

E

D
I
C
T
I
O
N
A
R
Y

178

to eat	*mee*·k-hui	mikhuy
to educate	yah·*chah*·chee	yachachiy
education	*yah*·chai	yachay
eggs	*roon*·too	runtu
to elect	*ahk*·lyai	akllay
electric light	loos	lus
to embarrass	p'en·*kah*·kui	p'inqakuy
embarrassed	p'en·*kahs*·kah	p'inqasqa
empire	tah-wahn-teen·*soo*·yoo	tawantinsuyu
empty	*ch'oo*·sahkh	ch'usaq
end	*too*·kui	tukuy
English	*een*·lees	inlis
to enjoy oneself	oo-sah·*chee*·kui	usachikuy
enough	chai·*lyah*·nyah	chayllaña
to enter	*hai*·kui	haykuy
to entertain	k'o·too·*ree*·chee	q'uturichiy
every	lyoo	lliw
everyone	lyoo·*neen*·koo	lliwninku
everything	*lyah*·pah	llapa
everywhere	mai·*pee*·pahs	maypipas
exact(ly)	*k'ah*·pahkh	k'apak
to exchange (products)	ch-*hah*·lai	chhalay
to exhibit	ree-koo·*ree*·chee	rikurichiy
to exist	kai	kay
to expect	*soo*·yai	suyay
expensive	*ahn*·chah chah·*nee*·yokh	ancha chaniyuq
to explain	yah·*chah*·chee	yachachiy

F

to fall	*oor*·mai	urmay
family	fah·*mee*·lyah	phamilla
famous	rekh·*sees*·kah	riqsisqa
far	*kah*·roo	karu
farm	*chahkh*·rah	chakra
farmer	*chahkh*·rah *roo*·nah	chakra runa
farmyard	*kahn*·chah	kancha
fast (movement)	p-hah·*wai*·lyah	phawaylla
fast (passage of time)	rah·*too*·lyah	ratulla
fat (grease)	*wee*·rah	wira
fault	*hoo*·chah	hucha
fava beans	*hah*·wahs	hawas
fear	mahn·*chah*·kui	manchakuy
to feed	*kah*·rai	qaray

English	Pronunciation	Quechua
to feel (sentiments)	*lyahkh·*lyai	llakllay
to feel (touch)	*lyah·*mee	llamiy
fence	*ken·*chah	qincha
festival	*rai·*mee	raymi
to fetch	poo·*sah·*mui	pusamuy
fever	*roo·*p-hah	rupha
few	*pee·*see	pisi
fiancé/fiancée	*oor·*pee	urpi
field (cultivated)	*chahkh·*rah	chakra
fight/to fight	ow·kah·*nah·*kui	awqanakuy
to fill	*hoon·*t'ai	hunt'ay
to find (something lost)	*tah·*ree	tariy
to finish	*too·*kui	tukuy
fire	*nee·*nah	nina
first	*nyow·*pahkh	ñawpaq
flashlight	k'ahn·*chah·*nah	k'anchana
flat (adj)	*p'ahl·*tah	p'alta
flat place	*pahm·*pah	pampa
flea	*pee·*kee	piki
flower	*t'ee·*kah	t'ika
flour	*hah·*k'oo	hak'u
to fly	*p-hah·*wai	phaway
fog	*pah·*chah *p-hoo·*yoo	pacha phuyu
to follow	*kah·*tee	qatiy
food	*mee·*k-hoo·*nah	mikhuna
foreigner	*hah·*wah *roo·*nah	hawa runa
forest	*mahlly·*kee *mahlly·*kee	mallki mallki
forever	*wee·*nyai·*pah·*chah	wiñaypacha
to forget	*kon·*kai	qunqay
to forgive	pahm·*pah·*chai	pampachay
fort/fortress	poo·*kah·*rah	pukara
fortune teller	*wah·*tokh	watuq
free (at liberty)	*kes·*pee	qispi
free (no cost)	*yahn·*kahn	yanqan
to freeze	*kah·*sai	qasay
friend	rekh·*see·*nah·kokh·*mah·*see	riqsinakuqmasi
from	·*mahn·*tah	-manta

> I'm from Cuzco.
> kos·ko·*mahn·*tah *kah·*nee   Qusqu-manta kani.

full (after a meal)	sahkh·*sahs·*kah	saksasqa
full (complete)	*hoon·*t'ah	hunt'a
to have fun	koo·*see·*kui	kusikuy
future	*hah·*mokh *pah·*chah	hamuq pacha

G

game	pookh·lyai	pukllay
garbage	k'o·pah	q'upa
garden (flower)	pow·kahr	pawqar
garden (fruit)	moo·yah	muya
garlic	ah·hoos	ahus
gate	hai·koo·nah	haykuna
to gather	pah·lyai	pallay
genuine	che·kahkh	chiqaq
to get lost	cheen·kai	chinkay
gift	ree·koo·chee·kui	rikuchikuy
girl	see·pahs	sipas
girlfriend	yah·nah·sah	yanasa
to give	koy	quy
to give birth (humans)	wah·chah·kui	wachakuy
to give birth (animals)	wah·chai	wachay
glass	kes·pee	qispi
to go	ree	riy
to go away	ree·pui	ripuy

> Get lost! Go away!
> *lyokh·see! ree·pui!*   ¡Lluqsiy! ¡Ripuy!

God	yah·yah	Yaya
gold	ko·ree	quri
good (adj)	ah·lyeen	allin

> Good afternoon.
> *wee·nahs tahr·dees*   Winas tardis.
>
> Good evening/night.
> *wee·nahs noo·chees*   Winas nuchis.
>
> Good morning.
> *wee·noos dee·yahs*   Winus diyas.
>
> Goodbye.
> *teen·koo·nahn·chees·kah·mah*   Tinkunanchiskama.

grass	k'ah·choo	q'achu
grave (tomb)	ah·yah sahn·k·hah	aya sankha
great (size)	hah·toon	hatun
great (quality)	koo·sah koo·sah	kusa kusa
to grow	wee·nyai	wiñay
guest	kor·pah	qurpa
guide (person)	nyahn·tah rekh·see·chekh	ñanta riqsichiq

H

hair (of body/animal)	*soo*·p-hoo	*suphu*
hair (of head)	*chookh*·chah	*chukcha*
half	*koos*·kahn	*kuskan*
to halt (oneself)	*sah*·yai	*sayay*
to halt (someone else)	sah·*yah*·chee	*sayachiy*
handbag	*ch'oos*·pah	*ch'uspa*
handsome	*soo*·mahkh	*sumaq*
hand-woven	mah·*kee*·wahn ah·*wahs*·kah	*makiwan awasqa*
happy	*koo*·see • koo·*sees*·kah	*kusi* • *kusisqa*
hard (difficult)	*sah*·sah	*sasa*
to have	kai	*kay*
he	pai	*pay*
to heal	*hahm*·pee	*hampiy*
healer	*hahm*·pekh	*hampiq*
health	k-*hah*·lee kai	*qhali kay*
to hear	oo·*yah*·ree	*uyariy*
to heat	*roo*·p-hai	*ruphay*
heaven	*hah*·nahkh *pah*·chah	*hanaq pacha*
heavy	*lyah*·sah	*llasa*
to help	yah·*nah*·pai	*yanapay*

Help me!	
yah·nah·pah·*wai*!	¡Yanapawáy!

herb	*ko*·rah	*qura*
herbalist	ko·*rah*·wahn *kahm*·pekh	*qurawan qampiq*
here	*kai*·pee	*kaypi*

Hey!	
yow!	¡Yaw!

high	*soo*·nee	*suni*
hike/to hike	*poo*·ree	*puriy*
hill	or·*ko*·chah	*urqucha*
to hire	ahl·*kee*·lai	*alkilay*
to hold	*hah*·p'ee	*hap'iy*
hole	*t'o*·ko	*t'uqu*
holiday	p-*hees*·tah	*phista*
home	*wah*·see ai·lyoo	*wasi ayllu*
honest	*soo*·mahkh	*sumaq*
	kow·sai·*nee*·yokh	*kawsayniyuq*
honey	ah·*nyah*·kah	*añaka*
honeycomb	lah·*chee*·*wah*·nah	*lachiwana*
hope	*soo*·yai	*suyay*

I

horrible	mee·lyai	millay
horse	kah·wah·lyoo	kawallu
to ride a horse	see·lyah·kui	sillakuy
hospital	hahm·pee·nah wah·see	hampina wasi
hot	roo·p-hah	rupha
to be hot (person)	roo·p-hah·ree	ruphariy
house	wah·see	wasi
how	ee·mai·nah	imayna
how much	hai·k'ahn	hayk'an
to hug	mah·k'ah·lyee	mak'alliy
to hug each other	mah·k'ah·lyee·nah·kui	mak'allinakuy
humankind	roo·nah	runa
to be hungry	yahr·kai	yarqay
to hurt	nah·nai	nanay

I

I	no·kah • nyo·kah	nuqa • ñuqa
ice	ch-hoo·lyoon·koo	chhullunku
if	see·choos	sichus
ill	on·kos·kah	unqusqa
to imitate	kah·tee·chee·kui	qatichikuy
immediately	koo·nah·lyahn	kunallan
important	chah·nee·yokh	chaniyuq
in	·pee	-pi
in a hurry	ah·poo·rahs·kah	apurasqa
Inca	een·kah	inka
(to become) infected	ch'oo·pui	ch'upuy
(to become) inflamed	poon·kee	punkiy
to inform	wee·lyai	willay
injury	k'ee·ree	k'iri
inside	oo·k·hoo·pee	ukhupi
instructor	yah·chah·chekh	yachachiq
intelligent	yah·chai·nee·yokh	yachayniyuq
to introduce (a person)	rekh·see·chee	riqsichiy
island	wah·t'ah	wat'a
itch (sensation)	sekh·see	siqsiy

J

jar	oor·poo	urpu
job	lyahn·k'ah·nah	llank'ana
to join	hookh·lyah·kui	hukllakuy
joke	chahn·sah	chansa
to joke	chahn·sah·kui	chansakuy
joker (comedian)	ah·see·chee·kokh	asichikuq

journey	kah·roo poo·ree	karu puriy
juice	hee·lyee	hilli
to jump	p'ee·tai	p'itay
jungle	yoon·kah	yunka

K

to keep	wah·kai·chai	waqaychay
to keep something for someone else	choo·rah·pui	churapuy
key	p'oo·tee • lyah·wee	p'uti • llawi
to kick	hai·t'ai	hayt'ay
to kill	wah·nyoo·chee	wañuchiy
kind (nice)	k-hoo·yah·kokh	khuyakuq
kind (type)	reekh·ch'ahkh	rikch'aq
to kiss	moo·ch'ai	much'ay
kitchen	koo·see·nah	kusina
knapsack	k'e·pee	q'ipi
knife	koo·choo·nah	kuchuna
to know (a fact)	yah·chai	yachay
to know (people or places)	rekh·see	riqsiy

L

lake	ko·chah	qucha
land	ahly·pah	allpa
language	ree·mai • see·mee	rimay • simi
large	hah·toon	hatun
last	kai·nah	qayna
late	tai·ree	tayri
to be late	tai·ree·yai	tayriyay
to laugh	ah·see	asiy
lazy	ke·lyah	qilla
leader	kah·mah·chekh	kamachiq
to lead	poo·sai	pusay
to learn	yah·chai	yachay
leather	kah·rah	qara
to leave (go away)	lyokh·see	lluqsiy
to leave something	sah·kay	saqiy
to be left over (in excess)	poo·chui	puchuy
left (not right)	lyo·k'e	lluq'i
left-handed	lyo·k'en·choo	lluq'inchu
to lend (durable items)	mah·nyai	mañay
to lend (consumables/ money)	mah·nui	manuy
to lend a hand	ai·nee	ayniy

ENGLISH – QUECHUA DICTIONARY

letter	kel·kah	qilqa
liar	lyoo·lyah	llulla
to lie (be untruthful)	lyoo·lyah·kui	llullakuy
to lie down	see·ree	siriy
life	kow·sai	kawsay
light (in weight)	ch-hah·lyah	chhalla
light (illumination)	k'ahn·chai	k'anchay
to like	moo·nai	munay
like (like this)	hee·nah	hina
liquor	trah·woo	trawu
to listen	oo·yah·ree	uyariy
little (small)	hoo·ch'ui	huch'uy
a little bit	pee·see pee·see·lyah	pisi pisilla
to live	kow·sai	kawsay
to live in	tee·yai	tiyay
lock	kahn·dah·roo·wahn	kandaruwan
	wees·k'ai	wisq'ay
to lock	wees·k'ah·nah	wisq'ana
long (length)	sui·t'oo	suyt'u
to look/look after	k-hah·wai	qhaway
to look for	mahs·k-hai	maskhay
to look like	reekh·ch'ah·kui	rikch'akuy
loose	wah·yah	waya
lost	cheen·kahs·kah	chinkasqa
a lot (quantity)	ahs·k-hah	askha
love/to love (affection)	k-hoo·yai	khuyay
love/to love (want/desire)	moo·nai	munay
love/to love (intense)	wai·lyui	waylluy
to (be in) love	son·ko too·pah·chee	sunqu tupachiy
to (fall in) love	moo·nah·nah·kui	munanakuy
to (fall in) love (intense)	wai·lyoo·nah·kui	wayllunakuy
lover	moo·nahkh • wai·lyokh	munaq • waylluq
luck	sah·mee	sami
lucky	sah·mee·yokh	samiyuq
lunch	ahl·moo·sai	almusay

M

made of	·mahn·tah	-manta
made of stone	roo·mee·mahn·tah	rumi-manta
main road	hah·toon nyahn	hatun ñan
main square	plah·sah	plasa
to make	roo·wai	ruway
man	k-hah·ree	qhari
mankind	roo·nah	runa
many	ahs·k-hah	askha

N

map	*mah·pah*	mapa
market	*k-hah·too • plah·sah*	qhatu • plasa
marriage	*kah·sah·rah·kui*	kasarakuy
marvellous	*ahn·chah soo·mahkh*	ancha sumaq
Mass (Catholic)	*mee·sah*	misa
match (sport)	*pookh·lyai*	pukllay
match (to light fires)	*foos·poo·roo*	phuspuru
to matter	*chah·nee·yokh kai*	chaniyuq kay

> It doesn't matter.
> *mah·nahn ee·mah·nahn·pahs·choo* — Manan imananpaschu.
>
> What's the matter?
> *ee·mah·tahkh soo·see·dee·soon·kee?* — ¿Imataq susidisunki?

mayor	*ahl·kahl·dee*	alkaldi
medicine	*hahm·pee*	hampi
medium	*tahkh·sah*	taksa
to meet	*teen·kui*	tinkuy
to meet up with	*too·pai*	tupay
menu	*mee·noo*	minu
message	*wee·lyah·chee·kui*	willachikuy
middle (in the)	*chow·peen·pee*	chawpinpi
milk	*lee·chee*	lichi
mirror	*leer·poo*	lirpu
to miss (person)	*wah·too·kui*	watukuy
mistake (make a)	*pahn·tai*	pantay
to mix	*tahkh·roy*	taqruy
money	*kol·ke*	qulqi
month	*kee·lyah*	killa
mosquito net	*moos·kee·tee·roo*	muskitiru
moon	*kee·lyah*	killa
more	*ahs·wahn*	aswan
more or less	*yah·kah*	yaqa
much	*ahn·chah*	ancha
mud	*t'oo·roo*	t'uru
music	*moo·see·kah*	musika
musician	*moo·see·koo*	musiku

N

name	*soo·tee*	suti
to name	*soo·tee·chai*	sutichay
narrow	*k'eekh·lyoo*	k'ikllu
nation	*lyahkh·tah*	llaqta
nature	*kow·sai pah·chah*	kawsay pacha
near	*sees·pah • kai·lyah*	sispa • qaylla

neck	*koon·kah*	*kunka*
necklace	*wahl·kah*	*walqa*
to need	*moo·nai*	*munay*
needle (sewing)	*ah·woo·hah*	*awuha*
needle (large)	*yow·ree*	*yawri*
neighbour	*wah·see·mah·see*	*wasi-masi*
never	*mah·nah hai·k'ahkh·pahs*	*mana hayk'aqpas*
new	*moo·sokh*	*musuq*
news	*wee·lyai·koo·nah*	*willaykuna*
next (following)	*hah·mokh • kah·tekh*	*hamuq • qatiq*
next to	*wahkh·tahn·pee*	*waqtanpi*
nice	*ah·lyeen*	*allin*
nickname	*k·hoo·yai soo·tee*	*khuyay suti*
night	*too·tah • ch'ee·see*	*tuta • ch'isi*
noise	*rokh·yah*	*ruqya*
none	*mah·nah*	*mana*
	ch'oo·lyah·lyah·pahs •	*ch'ullallapas •*
	mah·nah mai·ken	*mana mayqin*
north	*wee·chai*	*wichay*
nothing	*mah·nahn ee·mah·pahs*	*manan imapas*
not yet	*mah·nah·rahkh*	*manaraq*
now	*koo·nahn*	*kunan*

O

ocean	*ko·chah·mah·mah*	*quchamama*
of (poss)	*·kh • ·pah*	*-q • -pa*
of course	*ree·kee*	*riki*
often	*nyah·tahkh·nyah·tahkh*	*ñataq-ñataq*
old (age)	*mah·choo*	*machu*
old (worn out)	*t·han·tah*	*thanta*
on	*·pee*	*-pi*

> It's on the table.
> mee·*sah*·pee *kah*·shahn   *Misa-pi kashan.*

one	*hokh*	*huq*
onions	*see·wee·lyah*	*siwilla*
only	*·lyah*	*-lla*
open	*kee·chahs·kah*	*kichasqa*
to open	*kee·chai*	*kichay*
opinion	*hah·moo·t'ai*	*hamut'ay*
or	*ee·chah • oo·tahkh*	*icha • utaq*
to organise	*ah·lyee·chai*	*allichay*
original	*kahkh kee·keen*	*kaq kikin*
other	*hokh*	*huq*

P

Ouch!		
ah·chah·*kow*!		¡Achakáw!

outside	*hah*·wah	hawa
over	*hah*·wahn	hawan
overcoat	p'ees·*too*·nah	p'istuna
to owe (money)	*mah*·noo kai	manu kay
owl	*too*·koo	tuku
owner	*dui*·nyoo	duyñu

P

package	*k'e*·pee	q'ipi
pain	*nah*·nai	nanay
painkillers	*nah*·nai t-ha·*nee*·chekh	nanay thanichiq
to paint	*lyoo*·see	llusiy
painter	*lyoo*·sekh	llusiq
pants	pahn·*tah*·loon	pantalun
paper	*rah*·p'ah • *rah*·p-hee	rap'a • raphi
park	pook·*lyah*·nah *pahm*·pah	pukllana pampa
party	*fees*·tah	phista
to pass (hand to)	*hai*·wai	hayway
to pass (on the street)	*pah*·sai	pasay
to pass (cross a bridge/river)	*cheem*·pai	chimpay
passenger	pah·sah·*hee*·roo	pasahiru
past (remote, undefined time)	*oo*·nai • *nyow*·pah	unay • ñawpa
path	nyahn	ñan
patient (adj)	*lyah*·k-hee	llakhi
to pay	koy • *pah*·gai	quy • pagay
payment	*pah*·goo	pagu
peace	*kah*·see *kow*·sai	qasi kawsay
peak (of a mountain)	*poon*·tah	punta
peas	ahl·*weer*·hahs	alwirhas
pen/pencil	kel·*kah*·nah	qilqana
people	roo·nah·*koo*·nah	runakuna
perhaps	ee·chah·pahs·*chah*	ichapaschá
person	*roo*·nah	runa
pharmacy	hahm·*pee*·yokh *wah*·see	hampiyuq wasi
photo	*foo*·too	phutu
photographer	*foo*·too kor·kokh	phutu qurquq
to pick up (lift)	ho·*kah*·ree	huqariy
to pick up (gather, collect)	*pah*·lyai	pallay

188

English	Pronunciation	Quechua
piece	*ahkh*·no • *k'ookh*·moo	aqnu • k'ukmu
pill	pahs·*tee*·lyah	pastilla
pillow	*sow*·nah	sawna
place	*pah*·chah	pacha
plane	ah·*wee*·yoon	awiyun
plant	*ko*·rah • *yoo*·rah	qura • yura
to plant (trees)	*mahly*·kee	mallkiy
to plant (sow)	*tahr*·pui	tarpuy
to plant (vegetables)	*yoo*·rai	yuray
plate	*p'oo*·koo	p'uku
to play (games or sport)	*pookh*·lyai	pukllay
to play (music)	wah·*kah*·chee	waqachiy
playing field (sport)	pookh·*lyah*·nah	pukllana
	pahm·pah	pampa
plenty	*ahs*·k-hah	askha
pocket	wool·*see*·koo	wulsiku
poem	hah·*rah*·wee	harawi
police	wahr·*dee*·yah	wardiya
pond	*ko*·chah	qucha
poor/poor person	*wahkh*·chah	wakcha
possible	ah·tee·*nah*·lyah	atinalla
pot	*mahn*·kah	manka
pottery	*rahkh*·ch'ee	raqch'i
poverty	*wahkh*·chah kai	wakcha kay
power (ability)	*ah*·tee	atiy
power (strength)	*kahly*·pah	kallpa
powerful (rich/influential)	*k-hah*·pahkh	qhapaq
powerful (dominant)	ah·*tee*·pahkh	atipaq
to pray	mah·*nyah*·kui	mañakuy
to prefer	*moo*·nai	munay
pregnant (humans)	weekh·*sah*·yokh	wiksayuq
pregnant (animals)	*chee*·choo	chichu
to prepare	kah·*mah*·ree	kamariy
present (gift)	ree·k-hoo·*chee*·kui	rikhuchikuy
present (now)	*koo*·nahn • *kah*·nahn	kunan • kanan
pretty	*soo*·mahkh	sumaq
price (fair price)	*chah*·neen	chanin
probably	ee·*chah*·pahs	ichapas
to protect	ah·*mah*·chai	amachay
to pull	*ai*·sai	aysay
pure (water)	*ch'oo*·yah	ch'uya
purse with shoulder strap	*ch'oos*·pah	ch'uspa
to push	*tahn*·kai	tanqay
to put	*choo*·rai	churay

Q

Quechua speakers	*roo·*nah	runa
Quechua	roo·nah·*see*·mee	runasimi
question	tah·*poo*·nah	tapuna
to question	*tah·*pui	tapuy
quick	p-*hah*·wahkh • *oot*·k-hahkh	phawaq • utqhaq
quickly (motion)	p-hah·*wai*·lyah • oos·k-*hai*·lyah	phawaylla • usqhaylla
quickly (time)	rah·*too*·lyah	ratulla
quiet (silence)	ch'een	ch'in
quinoa (Andean grain)	*keen*·wah • *kyoo*·nyah	kinwa • kiwña

R

race (contest)	p-*hah*·wai	phaway
radio	rah·*dee*·yoo	radiyu
rain	*pah*·rah	para
to rain	*pah*·rai	paray
raw (uncooked)	*hahn*·koo	hanku
to read	*lee*·yee • nyah·*ween*·chai	liyiy • ñawinchay
ready	kah·mah·*rees*·kah	kamarisqa
real (genuine)	*che*·kahkh	chiqaq
reason	·*rai*·koo	-rayku
to receive	*chahs*·kee	chaskiy
recently	*chai*·rahkh	chayraq
to recognise	*rekh*·see	riqsiy
to refund	koo·tee·*chee*·pui	kutichipuy
to refuse	*ah*·mah nee	ama niy
region	*soo*·yoo	suyu
to regret	nah·nah·*chee*·kui	nanachikuy
to reject	*ah*·mah nee	ama niy
to relax	*how*·kay	hawkay
to remain	k-*he*·pai	qhipay
to remember	*yoo*·yai	yuyay
remote	*kah*·roo *kah*·roo	karu karu
to rent	ahl·*kee*·lai	alkilay
to repeat	koo·*tee*·pai	kutipay
to respect	yoo·*pai*·chai	yupaychay
rest/to rest (relax)	*sah*·mai	samay
rest (remaining)	*wah*·keen	wakin
restaurant	mee·*k-hoo*·nah *wah*·see	mikhuna wasi
restroom	hees·p'ah·*koo*·nah	hisp'akuna
to return (come back)	koo·*tee*·mui	kutimuy
rice	*ah*·roos	arus
to ride (a horse)	see·*lyah*·kui	sillakuy

right (correct)	chah·neen	chanin
right (not left)	pah·nyah	paña
ring (jewellery)	see·wee	siwi
ripe	po·kos·kah	puqusqa
river	mah·yoo	mayu
road	nyahn	ñan
to rob	soo·wah·kui	suwakuy
rock (stone)	roo·mee	rumi
rope	wahs·k-hah	waskha
round	moo·yoo	muyu
rubbish	k'o·pah	q'upa
rug	kom·pee	qumpi
ruins	nyow·pah lyahkh·tah • poo·roon lyahkh·tah	ñawpa llaqta • purun llaqta
rule	kah·mah·chee	kamachiy
to run	p-hah·wai	phaway

S

sad	lyah·kees·kah	llakisqa
safe	k-hah·lee·lyah	qhalilla
salt	kah·chee	kachi
same	kee·kee	kiki
sand	ah·ko	aqu
to save (a person)	kes·pee·chee	qispichiy
to say	nee	niy
school	yah·chai wah·see	yachay wasi
scissors	koo·choo·nah	kuchuna
sea	ko·chah·mah·mah	quchamama
to search	mahs·k-hai	maskhay
seat	tee·yah·nah	tiyana
to see	k-hah·wai	qhaway
seed	moo·hoo	muhu
to select	ahkh·lyai	akllay
to sell	been·dee	bindiy
to sell at a market/ fair/stand	k-hah·tui	qhatuy
to send a person (on an errand)	kah·chai	kachay
to separate	t'ah·kai • rah·kee	t'aqay • rakiy
to serve food	kah·rai	qaray
to sew	see·rai	siray
shade/shadow	lyahn·t-hoo	llanthu
to shake hands	lyah·mee·yui	llamiyuy
shampoo	chahm·poo	champu
to share one's food/drink	mah·lyee·chee	mallichiy

to shave	p'ahkh·lai	p'aqlay
shawl	lyeekh·lyah	lliklla
she	pai	pay
shelf	choo·rah·ree·nah	churarina
shine	k'ahn·chai	k'anchay
shop	teen·dah	tinda
short	tahkh·sah	taksa
to shout	kah·pah·ree	qapariy
show	k-hah·wah·chee	qhawachiy
shut	wees·k'ahs·kah	wisq'asqa
to shut	wees·k'ai	wisq'ay
sickness/to get sick	on·koy	unquy
side	keen·rai	kinray
sign	oo·nahn·chah	unancha
to sign (a document)	soo·tee sel·k'oy	suti silq'uy
signature	sel·k'o	silq'u
silent	ch'een	ch'in
silver	kol·ke	qulqi
similar	hee·nah	hina
to sing	tah·kee	takiy
singer	tah·kekh	takiq
single man	mah·nah wahr·mee·yokh	mana warmiyuq
single woman	mah·nah qo·sah·yokh	mana qusayuq
single (unique)	ch'oo·lyah	ch'ulla
to sit	tee·yai	tiyay
size/to size	sah·yai	sayay
sky	hah·nahkh pah·chah	hanaq pacha
sky blue	t'okh·rah ahn·kahs	t'uqra anqas
to sleep	poo·nyui	puñuy
sleepy	poo·nyui ai·sai	puñuy aysay
to slide	soo·chui	suchuy
slowly	ah·lyee·lyah·mahn·tah	allillamanta
small	hoo·ch'ui	huch'uy
to smell	moos·k·hee	muskhiy
to smile	ah·see·ree·kui	asirikuy
smoke	q'oos·nyee	q'usñi
to smoke (a cigarette)	pee·tai	pitay
smooth	syookh	siwk
to sneeze	ah·ch·hee	achhiy
snow/to snow	ree·t'ee	rit'i
so	chai hee·nah·kah • kai·nah·tah	chay hinaqa • kaynata
soap	hah·woon	hawun
soft	lyahm·p'oo	llamp'u
solid	ch'ee·lah • choo·choo	ch'ila • chuchu
some (animate object)	wah·keen·koo·nah·lyah	wakinkunalla

some (inanimate object)	wah·kee·wah·kee·lyan	wakiwakillan
someone	pee·pahs	pipas
something	ee·mah·pees • ee·mah·pahs	imapis • imapas
sometimes	mai·nee·lyahn·pee	maynillanpi
song (sad)	tah·kee • hah·rah·wee	taki • harawi
soon	koo·nah·lyan	kunallan

Sorry.
dees·peen·sah·yoo·wai   Dispinsayuway.

sound	sui·nai	suynay
Spanish	kahs·tee·lyah·noo	kastillanu
to speak	ree·mai	rimay
speedy	oos·k·hakh	usqhaq
spindle (for spinning)	poos·kah	puska
spring (water)	pookh·yoo	pukyu
square (shape)	tah·wah k'oo·choo·yokh	tawa k'uchuyuq
square (town)	plah·sah	plasa
stairs	pah·tah pah·tah	pata pata
to stand	sah·yai	sayay
stars	koy·lyoor • ch'ahs·kah	quyllur • ch'aska
to start	kah·lyah·ree	qallariy
to stay (remain)	k·he·pai	qhipay
to steal	soo·wai	suway
steam	wahkh·see	waksi
steep	sah·yahkh	sayaq
to step	t·haht·kee	thatkiy
step on	sah·rui	saruy
stone	roo·mee	rumi
to stop (oneself)	sah·yai	sayay
to stop (someone else)	sah·yah·chee	sayachiy
storm	lyokh·lyahh pah·rah	lluqlla para
story	wee·lyah·kui	willakuy
straight	syook	siwk
stranger	mah·nah rek·sees·kah	mana riqsisqa
stream	mah·yoo·chah • oo·noo hai·kokh	mayucha • unu haykuq
street	nyahn • kah·lyee	ñan • kalli
strength	kahly·pah	kallpa
string	k'ai·too	q'aytu
strong (solid)	choo·choo	chuchu
strong (durable)	kah·kah	qaqa
strong (person)	seen·chee	sinchi
student	yah·chai moo·nahkh	yachay munaq

stupid	*mah*·nah ah·*lyeen* yoo·yai·*nee*·yokh	*mana allin yuyayniyuq*
to succeed	ah·*lyeen*·wahn *lyokh*·see	*allinwan lluqsiy*
to suffer	*nyah*·kai	*ñakay*
sugar	*mees*·k'ee • ah·*soo*·kahr	*misk'i • asukar*
suitcase	mah·*lee*·tah	*malita*
sunlight	*roo*·p·hai	*ruphay*
sunrise	*een*·tee lyee·pee·*pee*·mui • *lyokh·see*·mui	*inti llipipimuy • lluqsimuy*
sunset	ch'ee·see·yai·pui • een·tee·*yai*·kui	*ch'isiyapuy • intiyaykuy*
to sweep	*pee*·chai	*pichay*
sweet	*mees*·k'ee	*misk'i*
to swim	*wai*·t'ai	*wayt'ay*

table	*wahm*·pahr	*wampar*
to take	*ah*·pai	*apay*
to take (on your back)	*k'e*·pee	*q'ipiy*
talk	*ree*·mai	*rimay*
tall	*hah*·toon	*hatun*
tambourine	*teen*·yah	*tinya*
to taste	mah·*lyee*	*malliy*
tasty	soo·*mahkh* • *mees*·k'ee	*sumaq • misk'i*
teacher	yah·*chah*·chekh • hah·*mow*·t'ah	*yachachiq • hamawt'a*
tear	*we*·ke	*wiqi*
teeth	*kee*·roo	*kiru*
to tell	*nee* • *wee*·lyai	*niy • willay*
temperature (fever)	roo·p·hai on·koy	*ruphay unquy*
temple	*mahn*·ko/yoo·*pai*·chai wah·*see*	*manqu/yupaychay wasi*
terrible	*mah*·nah ah·*lyeen*	*mana allin*
to thank	ah·*nyai*·chai • sool·*pai* nee	*añaychay • sulpáy niy*

Thank you.
ah·*nyai·chai*·kee • sool·*pai*   *Añaychayki.* • *Sulpáy.*

that	*chai* • *ahn*·chai	*chay • anchay*
that over there	*chah*·hai • hah·*kai*	*chahay • haqay*
them	pai·*koo*·nah	*paykuna*
then (at that time)	chai *pah*·chah	*chay pacha*
there	*chai*·pee	*chaypi*
they	pai·*koo*·nah	*paykuna*

ENGLISH – QUECHUA DICTIONARY

English	Pronunciation	Quechua
thief	soo·wah	suwa
thin (skinny)	too·lyoo	tullu
to think	yoo·yai	yuyay
thirst	ch'ah·kee	ch'akiy
thirsty	ch'ah·kees·kah	ch'akisqa
this	kai	kay
thought	yoo·yai	yuyay
to tie	wah·tai	watay
tight	mah·t'ee	mat'i
time	pah·chah	pacha
tin (of food)	lah·tah	lata
tin opener	lah·tah kee·chah·nah	lata kichana
tired	sai·k'oos·kah	sayk'usqa
today	koo·nahn p'oon·chai	kunan p'unchay
together	koos·kah	kuska
toilet	hees·p'ah·koo·nah	hisp'akuna
tomorrow	pah·kah·reen	paqarin
too	·pees • ·pahs	-pis • -pas

Me too.
no·kah·pees• nyo·kah·pahs | Ñuqa-pis.• Ñuqa-pas.

too much	chee·kah chee·kah	chika chika
torch	k'ahn·chah·nah	k'anchana
to touch	lyah·mee	llamiy
tourist	too·rees·tah	turista
towards/to	·mahn • ·tah	-man • -ta
towel	too·wah·lyah	tuwalla
town	lyahkh·tah	llaqta
track (path)	nyahn	ñan
to translate	t'eekh·rai	t'ikray
trash	k'o·pah	q'upa
to travel	ch'oo·sai • poo·ree	ch'usay • puriy
traveller	poo·rekh	puriq
tree	mahly·kee	mallki
to trek	kah·roo poo·ree	karu puriy
truck	kah·mee·yoon	kamiyun
true	che·kahkh	chiqaq

It's true!
che·kahkh·mee! | ¡Chiqaqmi!

| to trust | koon·p·hee·yai | kunphiyay |
| truth | che·kahkh | chiqaq |

to turn	moo·yoo·ree	*muyuriy*

Turn left.
lyo·*k'e*·mahn moo·*yoo*·ree — *Lluq'iman muyuriy.*

Turn right.
pah·*nyah*·mahn moo·*yoo*·ree — *Pañaman muyuriy.*

twice	ees·kai koo·tee	*iskay kuti*

U

under	pah·chahn	*pachan*
to understand	een·*teen*·dee	*intindiy*
universe	tekh·see·*moo*·yoo	*tiqsimuyu*
until	·*kah*·mah	*-kama*
up	hah·nahkh	*hanaq*
uphill	wee·chai	*wichay*
to be upset	p-hee·*nyah*·kui	*phiñakuy*
urgent	oos·*k-hai*·pahkh	*usqhaypaq*
useful	ah·lyeen	*allin*

V

vacation	sah·mai pah·chah	*samay pacha*
valley	k-hes·wah • wai·k'o	*qhiswa • wayq'u*
valuable	chah·*nee*·yokh	*chaniyuq*
value	chah·neen	*chanin*
vegetarian	mah·nah ai·chah mee·kokh	*mana aycha mikuq*
very	ahn·chah	*ancha*
village	lyahkh·tah	*llaqta*
to visit	wah·*too*·kui	*watukuy*

W

to wait	soo·yai	*suyay*
to walk	poo·ree	*puriy*
wall	per·kah	*pirqa*
to want	moo·nai	*munay*
warm	k'o·nyee	*q'uñi*
to warm up	k'o·*nyee*·kui	*q'uñikuy*
to warn	yoo·*yahm*·pai	*yuyampay*
to wash (clothes/hair)	t'ahkh·sai	*t'aqsay*
to wash (general, except clothes/hair)	mahkh·ch-hee	*maqchhiy*
to wash oneself (bathe)	ahr·*mah*·kui	*armakuy*

washing powder	dee·teer·*heen*·tee	ditirhinti
watch	k-*hah*·wai	qhaway
to watch	*ree*·looh	riluh
water	oo·noo • *yah*·koo	unu • yaku
waterfall	p-*hahkh*·chah	phaqcha
way (path)	nyahn	ñan
we (exclusive)	no·*kai*·koo	nuqayku
we (inclusive)	no·*kahn*·chees	nuqanchis
weak	*kahly*·pah wah·nyui	kallpa wañuy
to wear (clothes)	p'ah·chah·*lyee*·kui	p'achallikuy
to weave	ah·wai	away
wedding	kah·sah·*rah*·kui	kasarakuy
week	see·*mah*·nah	simana
to weigh	ai·sai	aysay
weight	*lyah*·sah	llasa
well	*ah*·lyeen	allin
west	*een*·tee cheen·*kai*·kui	inti chinkaykuy
wet	ho·k'o	huq'u

What?		
ee·mahn?		¿Iman?
What! (response to being called)		
hai!/*ee*·mah!		¡Hay!/¡Ima!
When?		
hai·k'*ahkh*?		¿Hayk'aq?
Where?		
mai·peen?		¿Maypin?
From where?		
mai·*mahn*·tahn?		¿Maymantan?
To where?		
mai·*tah*·tahkh?		¿Maytataq?
Which?		
mai·keen?		¿Mayqin?
Who?		
peen? (sg)/pee·*koo*·nahn? (pl)		¿Pin?/¿Pikunan?
Who is it?		
peen?		¿Pin?
Whose?		
pekh·pah?		¿Piqpa?
Why?		
ee·mah·*nahkh*·teen?		¿Imanaqtin?

Y

window	t'o·ko • ween·tah·nah	t'uqu • wintana
winter	chee·ree mee·t'ah	chiri mit'a
with	·wahn	-wan
with me	no·kah·wahn	nuqa-wan
woman	wahr·mee	warmi
wonderful	ahn·chah soo·mahkh	ancha sumaq
wood	k'oo·lyoo	k'ullu
wool	meely·mah	millma
word	ree·mai • see·mee	rimay • simi
to work	lyahn·k'ai	llank'ay
world	pah·chah • tekh·see·moo·yoo	pacha • tiqsimuyu
worried	lyah·kees·kah	llakisqa
to worship	yoo·pai·chai	yupaychay
worth (value)	chah·neen	chanin
to write	kel·kai	qilqay
wrong (mistaken)	pahn·tah	panta

Y

year	wah·tah	wata
you (sg)	kahn	qan
you (pl)	kahn·koo·nah	qankuna

Z

| zero | ch'oo·sahkh | ch'usaq |

A

achhiy	*ah·ch-hee*	to sneeze
aha	*ah·hah*	*chicha* (maize beer)
ahinaqa	*ah·hee·nah·kah*	so
akllay	*ahk·lyai*	to choose
aksidinti	*ahkh·see·deen·tee*	accident
akupana	*ah·koo·pah·nah*	sunset
alkaldi	*ahl·kahl·dee*	mayor
alkilay	*ahl·kee·lai*	to hire • to rent
almusay	*ahl·moo·sai*	to have lunch
allillamanta	*ah·lyee·lyah·mahn·tah*	slowly
allin	*ah·lyeen*	good • useful • well
allpa	*ahly·pah*	land • earth (soil)
ama niy	*ah·mah nee*	to refuse • to reject
amachay	*ah·mah·chai*	to protect
amisqa	*ah·mes·kah*	bored • boring
ancha	*ahn·chah*	much • very
apamuy	*ah·pah·mui*	to bring
apay	*ah·pai*	to take
apu	*ah·poo*	rich
apurasqa	*ah·poo·rahs·kah*	in a hurry
aqnu	*ahkh·no*	piece
aqu	*ah·ko*	sand
armakuy	*ahr·mah·kui*	to bathe • to wash oneself
arpha	*ahr·p-hah*	blind (adj)
as aslla	*ahs ahs·lyah*	a little bit
asirikuy	*ah·see·ree·kui*	to smile
asiti	*ah·see·tee*	oil (cooking)
asiy	*ah·see*	to laugh
askamalla	*ahs·kah·mah·lyah*	quickly • fast (time)
askha	*ahs·k-hah*	many • a lot of
asnay	*ahs·nai*	to smell
asukar	*ah·soo·kahr*	sugar
aswan	*ahs·wahn*	more
aswan allin	*ahs·wahn ah·lyeen*	better
aswan hatun	*ahs·wahn hah·toon*	bigger
atinalla	*ah·tee·nah·lyah*	possible
atipaq	*ah·tee·pahkh*	powerful
atipay	*ah·tee·pai*	to put up with
atiy	*ah·tee*	to be able • power • strength
away	*ah·wai*	to weave
awiyun	*ah·wee·yoon*	aeroplane
awtu	*ow·too*	car
awuha	*ah·woo·hah*	needle (sewing)
aya p'ampana	*ah·yah p'ahm·pah·nah*	cemetery
aya sankha	*ah·yah sahn·k-hah*	grave • tomb
aycha kurku	*ai·chah koor·koo*	body

ayllu	*ai·lyoo*	community • family
ayniy	*ai·nee*	to help out
ayqi	*ai·ke*	to exit • to leave
aysay	*ai·sai*	to pull • to stretch

B

bañu	*bah·nyoo*	bathroom • toilet
bindiy	*been·dee*	to sell

CH

chahay	*chah·hai*	that over there
chaka	*chah·kah*	bridge • thigh
chakra	*chahkh·rah*	farm • field (cultivated) • earth (soil)
chanin	*chah·neen*	fair price • value • worth • right • correct • true
chaniyuq	*chah·nee·yokh*	important • valuable
chaniyuq kay	*chah·nee·yokh kai*	to matter (be important)
chansa	*chahn·sah*	joke
chaskiy	*chahs·kee*	to receive
chawpinpi	*chow·peen·pee*	in the middle
chay	*chai*	that
chay hinaqa	*chai hee·nah·kah*	so
chay pacha	*chai pah·chah*	then • at that time
chayasqa	*chah·yahs·kah*	done (of food)
chayay	*chai·yai*	to arrive
chayllaña	*chai·lyah·nyah*	enough
chaymanta	*chai·mahn·tah*	besides (furthermore)
chaymantaqa	*chai·mahn·tah·kah*	afterwards
chaypachamanta	*chai·pah·chah·mahn·tah*	since then
chaypas	*chai·pahs*	although
chaypi	*chai·pee*	there
chayraq	*chai·rahkh*	recently
chimpapi	*cheem·pah·pee*	across (from)
chimpay	*cheem·pai*	to pass • to cross over
chinkasqa	*cheen·kahs·kah*	lost • hidden
chipchiy	*cheep·chee*	to shine (sun) • to illuminate
chiqanta	*che·kahn·tah*	straight
chiqaq	*che·kahkh*	truth • real • genuine
chiskasqa puriy	*chees·kahs·kah poo·ree*	to be lost
chiyay	*chee·yai*	to arrive
chuchu	*choo·choo*	solid • strong
chupi	*choo·pee*	soup
churanakuy	*choo·rah·nah·kui*	to argue
churapuy	*choo·rah·pui*	to keep something for someone else
churarina	*choo·rah·ree·nah*	shelf

churay	choo·rai	to put • to inject
chusi	choo·see	blanket
chuyk'ucha	chui·k'oo·chah	cup

CHH

chhalay	ch-hah·lai	to barter • to exchange
chhalla	ch-hah·lyah	light (in weight)
chhika	ch-hee·kah	plenty
chhika chhika	ch-hee·kah ch-hee·kah	too much • too many
chhulli	ch-hoo·lyee	influenza
chhullunku	ch-hoo·lyoon·koo	ice
chhuqay	ch-ho·kai	to push

CH'

ch'aka	ch'ah·kah	sore throat • hoarse
ch'aki	ch'ah·kee	dry
ch'akisqa	ch'ah·kees·kah	thirsty
ch'akiy	ch'ah·kee	to dry • to be thirsty • thirst
ch'aska	ch'ahs·kah	stars
ch'ikay	ch'ee·kai	sting (of bee/wasp)
ch'in	ch'een	quiet (silence) • silent
ch'iqmiy	ch'ekh·mee	to bother
ch'isiyay	ch'ee·see·yai	to get dark
ch'ulla	ch'oo·lyah	single (unique)
ch'unku	ch'oon·koo	crowd • group
ch'upuy	ch'oo·pui	to become infected
ch'usaq	ch'oo·sahkh	space • zero • empty
ch'usay	ch'oo·sai	to travel
ch'uspa	ch'oos·pah	small bag • handbag
ch'ustikuy	ch'oos·tee·kui	to undress
ch'uya	ch'oo·yah	clean • pure (of water)

D

Diyus	dee·yoos	God
duktur	dookh·toor	doctor

H

hamawt'a	hah·mow·t'ah	teacher • professor • community leader • wise
hampi	hahm·pee	drug • medicine
hampina wasi	hahm·pee·nah wah·see	hospital
hampiq	hahm·pekh	healer
hampiy	hahm·pee	to heal • to cure
hampiyuq wasi	hahm·pee·yokh wah·see	drugstore • pharmacy

hamuq	*hah*·mokh	next (following)
hamuy	*hah*·mui	to come
hanaq	*hah*·nahkh	up • above
hanaq pacha	*hah*·nahkh *pah*·chah	heaven • sky
hanku	*hahn*·koo	raw (uncooked)
hanq'ara	hahn·*k'ah*·rah	dish
hap'iy	*hah*·p'ee	to hold
haqay	*hah*·kai	that over there
harawi	hah·*rah*·wee	poem • song
hark'apay	hahr·*k'ah*·pai	to protect
hark'ay	*hahr*·k'ai	to prevent
hasp'ikuy	hahs·*p'ee*·kui	itch • to scratch
hatun	*hah*·toon	big • high • large • tall
hawa	*hah*·wah	outside
hawa runa	*hah*·wah *roo*·nah	foreigner
hawanpi	hah·*wahn*·pee	above
hawan	*hah*·wahn	over
hawapi	hah·*wah*·pee	outside
hawkay	*how*·kai	to relax
hayk'an	*hai*·k'ahn	how much
hayk'aq	*hai*·k'ahkh	when
haykuna	hai·*koo*·nah	gate
haykuy	*hai*·kui	to enter
hayway	*hai*·wai	to pass (hand to)
hina	*hee*·nah	similar • like this/that
hina kaqlla	*hee*·nah *kahkh*·lyah	permanent
hinaspa	hee·*nahs*·pah	besides (furthermore) • thus
hinastin	hee·*nahs*·teen	everywhere
hisp'akuna	hees·p'ah·*koo*·nah	toilet • restroom
hisp'akuy	hees·*p'ah*·kui	to urinate
hucha	*hoo*·chah	fault • sin
huchallikuy	hoo·chah·*lyee*·kui	to sin
huch'uy	*hoo*·ch'ui	small • little
huk'i	*hoo*·k'ee	corner (inside)
huklla	*hookh*·lyah	together
hukllakuy	hookh·*lyah*·kui	to join
hukllay	*hookh*·lyai	to mix
hunt'a	*hoon*·t'ah	full (complete)
hunt'asqa	*hoon*·t'ahs·kah	exact • exactly
huñiy	*hoo*·nyee	to allow • to permit
hup'a	*hoo*·p'ah	deaf
huq	hokh	one • another • other
huq ratuña	hokh rah·*too*·nyah	ago
huqariy	ho·*kah*·ree	to pick up (lift)
huqmanta	hokh·*mahn*·tah	again
huqnirayay	hokh·nee·*rah*·yai	to change (into something) • to become
huq'u	*ho*·k'o	damp • wet
hurquy	*hor*·koy	to take

I

icha	ee·chah	or
ichapas	ee·chah·pahs	probably
ichapaschá	ee·chah·pahs·chah	perhaps
imallapas	ee·mah·lyah·pahs	anything • something
iman	ee·mahn	what
imanaqtin	ee·mah·nahkh·teen	why
imayna	ee·mai·nah	how
iniy/iñiy	ee·nee/ee·nyee	to believe (religious)
inka	een·kah	Inca
inlis	een·lees	English
inlisa	een·lee·sah	church
intindiy	een·teen·dee	to understand
isanka	ee·sahn·kah	basket
iskay kuti	ees·kai koo·tee	twice
iskaynin	ees·kai·neen	both

K

kachay	kah·chai	to send (on an errand)
kalli	kah·lyee	street
kallpa	kahly·pah	strength
kallpa wañuy	kahly·pah wah·nyui	weak
-kama	·kah·mah	until
kamachiy	kah·mah·chee	to order • to rule
kamarikuy	kah·mah·ree·kui	to decide
kamarisqa	kah·mah·rees·kah	ready
kamariy	kah·mah·ree	to prepare
kambiyay	kahm·bee·yai	to change
kamisa	kah·mee·sah	shirt
kanallan	kah·nah·lyahn	immediately • very soon
kanasta	kah·nahs·tah	basket
kandaruwan wisq'ay	kahn·dah·roo·wahn wees·k'ai	to lock
kaniy	kah·nee	bite (of any creature)
kaq kikin	kahkh kee·keen	original
karu	kah·roo	far
karu llaqta	kah·roo lyahkh·tah	abroad
karu llaqta runa	kah·roo lyahkh·tah roo·nah	foreigner
karu puriy	kah·roo poo·ree	journey • trek
karru	kah·rroo	car • truck
kasarakuqmasi	kah·sah·rah·kokh·mah·see	fiancé • fiancée
kasarakuy	kah·sah·rah·kui	to marry • marriage • wedding
kastillanu	kahs·tee·lyah·noo	Spanish
katuliku	kah·too·lee·koo	Catholic

kawra	kow·rah	goat
kawsay pacha	kow·sai pah·chah	nature
kay	kai	to exist • to be • to have • this
kaynata	kai·nah·tah	so
kaypi	kai·pee	here
kichasqa	kee·chahs·kah	open
kichay	kee·chai	to open
kiki	kee·kee	same
killa	kee·lyah	month • moon
kinray	keen·rai	side
kinwa	keen·wah	quinoa (Andean grain)
kirpu	keer·poo	body
kuchuna	koo·choo·nah	knife • scissors
kuchuy	koo·chui	to cut
kunallan	koo·nah·lyan	immediately • very soon
kunan	koo·nahn	now • present (now)
kunan pacha	koo·nahn pah·chah	right now
kunphiyay	koon·p-hee·yai	to trust
kuntra	koon·trah	against
kura	koo·rah	priest
kurku	koor·koo	body
kusa	koo·sah	nice • right (interjection)
kusa kusa	koo·sah koo·sah	great (quality) • marvellous • wonderful
kusi	koo·see	happy
kusikuy	koo·see·kui	to have fun
kusisqa	koo·sees·kah	happy
kuska	koos·kah	side by side • together
kuskachakuy	koos·kah·chah·kui	to join
kutichipuy	koo·tee·chee·pui	to refund • compensation
kutichiy	koo·tee·chee	to answer
kutimuy	koo·tee·mui	to return (come back)
kutipay	koo·tee·pai	to repeat
kutuna	koo·too·nah	jacket (of a woman)
kwistay	kwees·tai	to cost

KH

khachuy	k-hah·chui	to bite (dog) • to bite off
kharka	k-hahr·kah	dirty
khumpa	k-hoom·pah	friend
khutu	k-hoo·too	frozen (solid)
khuyakuq	k-hoo·yah·kokh	kind (nice)
khuyay	k-hoo·yai	love/to love
khuyay suti	k-hoo·yai soo·tee	nickname

K'

k'akra	*k'ahk·rah*	ceramic
k'allma	*k'ahly·mah*	branch
k'anay	*k'ah·nai*	to burn • to set fire to
k'anchay	*k'ahn·chai*	to shine (sun) • to illuminate • light
k'apak	*k'ah·pahkh*	exact • exactly
k'aphra	*k'ah·p-hrah*	ceramic
k'awchi	*k'ow·chee*	jar
k'ikllu	*k'eek·lyoo*	narrow
k'iri	*k'ee·ree*	injury • wound
k'irikuy	*k'ee·ree·kui*	to wound
k'uchu	*k'oo·choo*	corner (outside)
k'ukmu	*k'ookh·moo*	piece
k'uku	*k'oo·koo*	short (in distance)
k'utuy	*k'oo·tui*	bite (insect) • to bite (hard things)

L

laranha	*lah·rahn·hah*	orange (fruit)
lata	*lah·tah*	can (of food)
lata kichana	*lah·tah kee·chah·nah*	can opener
lawa	*lah·wah*	soup
lintirna	*leen·teer·nah*	torch • flashlight
lirpu	*leer·poo*	mirror
liyiy	*lee·yee*	to read
lus	*loos*	electric light
luylu	*lui·loo*	clean

LL

-lla	*·lyah*	only
llakhi	*lyah·k-hee*	patient
llakisqa	*lyah·kees·kah*	sad • worried
llakllay	*lyahkh·lyai*	to sense • to feel
llamiy	*lyah·mee*	to feel (touch)
llamiyuy	*lyah·mee·yui*	to shake hands
llamp'u	*lyahm·p'oo*	soft
llank'ana	*lyahn·k'ah·nah*	job
llanthu	*lyahn·t-hoo*	shade • shadow
llapa	*lyah·pah*	everything • every • all
llapan	*lyah·pahn*	everyone
llapanku	*lyah·pahn·koo*	everyone
llaqta	*lyahkh·tah*	city • community • country • nation • town • village

llasa	lyah·sah	heavy • weight
llimpi	lyeem·pee	colour
lliw	lyoo	every • all • everything
lliwninku	lyoo·neen·koo	everyone
llulla	lyoo·lyah	liar
llullakuy	lyoo·lyah·kui	to lie (be untruthful)
llumpaq	lyoom·pahkh	pure • innocent
llumpay sumaq	lyoom·pai soo·mahkh	wonderful
llunch'iq	lyoon·ch'ekh	painter
lluq'i	lyo·k'e	left (not right)
lluq'inchu	lyo·k'en·choo	left-handed
lluqsiy	lyokh·see	to depart • to exit • to go away
llusiy	lyoo·see	to colour • to paint

M

machasqa/machaq	mah·chahs·kah/ mah·chahkh	drunk
machu	mah·choo	old (age)
machay	mah·chai	to get drunk
mahanakuy	mah·kah·nah·kui	fight • to fight
makiwan awasqa	mah·kee·wahn ah·wahs·kah	hand-woven
mak'allinakuy	mah·k'ah·lyee·nah·kui	to hug each other
mak'alliy	mah·k'ah·lyee	to hug
mak'as	mah·k'ahs	jar
malita	mah·lee·tah	luggage • suitcase
malqu	mahl·ko	chick
malliy	mah·lyee	to taste
malliyachiy	mah·lyee·yah·chee	to share one's food • to drink with someone
mallki mallki	mahly·kee mahly·kee	forest
mallkiy	mahly·kee	to plant
mama	mah·mah	mother • Mrs • Madam
-man	·mahn	towards • to
mana allin	mah·nah ah·lyeen	bad •
mana allin yuyayniyuq	mah·nah ah·lyeen yoo·yai·nee·yokh	stupid
mana mayqin	mah·nah mai·ken	none
mana qasiq	mah·nah kah·sekh	busy
mana qusayuq	mah·nah qo·sah·yokh	single woman
mana riqsisqa	mah·nah rek·sees·kah	stranger
mana warmiyuq	mah·nah wahr·mee·yokh	single man
manan imapas	mah·nahn ee·mah·pahs	nothing

QUECHUA – ENGLISH DICTIONARY

manan niy	mah·nahn nee	to deny
manaraq	mah·nah·rahkh	not yet
manchakuy	mahn·chah·kui	to be afraid • fear
manchay	mahn·chai	danger
manka	mahn·kah	pan • pot
-manta	·mahn·tah	from • made of
manu kay	mah·noo kai	to owe (money)
manuy	mah·nui	to lend (consumables/money)
mañakuy	mah·nyah·kui	to ask (for something) • to borrow • to pray
mañay	mah·nyai	to lend (durable items)
map'a	mah·p'ah	awful
maqanakuy	mah·kah·nah·kui	to argue
maqchhiy	mahkh·ch·hee	to wash (general, not clothes/hair)
masi	mah·see	companion • member (club)
maskhay	mahs·k·hai	to look for • to search
mat'i	mah·t'ee	tight
mat'isqa	mah·t'ees·kah	tight
maypin	mai·peen	where
maymantan	mai·mahn·tahn	from where
maytataq	mai·tah·tahkh	to where
mayqin	mai·keen	which
michiy	mee·chee	to pasture
mihuy	mee·hui	to eat • food • lunch
mikhuna wasi	mee·k·hoo·nah wah·see	restaurant
mik'i	mee·k'ee	slightly damp
millay	mee·lyai	ugly
millay millay	mee·lyai mee·lyai	horrible (appearance)
misa	mee·sah	Mass (Catholic worship service)
misk'i	mees·k'ee	sweet • delicious • tasty • honey • sugar
much'ay	moo·ch'ai	to kiss • to worship
muhu	moo·hoo	seed
munakuq	moo·nah·kokh	kind (nice)
munanakuy	moo·nah·nah·kui	to love (fall in)
munay	moo·nai	love • to love • to want • to desire • to prefer
munaq	moo·nahkh	lover
muskhiy	moos·k·hee	to smell
musqhuy	mos·k·hoy	dream • to dream
musuq	moo·sokh	new
muya	moo·yah	garden (fruit)
muyu	moo·yoo	round
muyuriy	moo·yoo·ree	to turn

N

nanachikuy	nah·nah·*chee*·kui	to regret • to resent
nanay	*nah*·nai	to hurt • physical pain
nanay thanichiq	*nah*·nai t-ha·*nee*·chekh	painkillers
naqha	*nah*·k-hah	ago
niy	nee	to say • to tell

Ñ

-ña	·nyah	already
ñakay	*nyah*·kai	to suffer
ñakariy	nyah·*kah*·ree	to suffer
ñan	nyahn	path • road • way
ñaña	*nyah*·nyah	friend (female friend to female) • sister (of woman)
ñanta riqsichiq	*nyahn*·tah rekh·*see*·chekh	guide (person)
ñapu	*nyah*·poo	ripe
ñaqch'a	*nyahkh*·ch'ah	comb
ñaqha	*nyah*·k-hah	ago
ñawinchay	nyah·*ween*·chai	to read
ñawpa	*nyow*·pah	past • ancient
ñawpa llaqta	*nyow*·pah *lyahkh*·tah	ruins
ñawpaq	*nyow*·pahkh	ahead • past • ancient
ñawpaq kaq	*nyow*·pahkh kahkh	first
ñawpaqta	*nyow*·pahkh·tah	before (time)
ñawsa	*nyow*·sah	blind (adj)
ñiqin	*nyeh*·ken	first

P

-pa	·pah	of
pacha	*pah*·chah	world • universe • space • time
pacha kuyuy	*pah*·chah koo·yui	earthquake
pacha phuyu	*pah*·chah p-*hoo*·yoo	fog
pachan	*pah*·chahn	under
pagu	*pah*·goo	payment
pallay	*pah*·lyai	to pick up • to collect
pampa	*pahm*·pah	countryside • flat place • floor • plain
pampachay	pahm·*pah*·chai	to forgive
pana/pani	*pah*·nah/*pah*·nee	friend (female friend to male) • sister (of man)
panta	*pahn*·tah	wrong • mistaken
pantalun	pahn·*tah*·loon	trousers
pantay	*pahn*·tai	to make a mistake

paña	pah·nyah	right (not left)
paqta	pahkh·tah	perhaps
para	pah·rah	rain
pasahiru	pah·sah·hee·roo	passenger
pasaq kutilla	pah·sahkh koo·tee·lyah	constantly • always
pasay	pah·sai	to pass (on the street)
pasayuy	pah·sah·yui	to enter
pastilla	pahs·tee·lyah	pill
pata	pah·tah	over • on
patapi	pah·tah·pee	above
phukuna waqra	p·hoo·koo·nah wahkh·rah	Andean horn
pin	peen	who
-pi	·pee	on • in • at
pichay	pee·chai	to clean • to sweep
pikaq	pee·kahkh	scorpion
piluta	pee·loo·tah	ball
pipas	pee·pahs	someone
piqpa	pekh·pah	whose
pirqa	per·kah	wall
pirqachay	per·kah·chai	to build
-pis	·pees	also • too • and
pisi	pee·see	few • little • scarce
pisi pisilla	pee·see pee·see·lyah	a little bit
pitay	pee·tai	to smoke (a cigarette)
plasa	plah·sah	plaza
prisisaqpaq	pree·see·sahkh·pahkh	urgent
puchuy	poo·chui	be left over (excess)
pukara	poo·kah·rah	fort • fortress
pukllana pampa	pook·lyah·nah pahm·pah	park • playing field
pukllapayay	pook·lyah·pah·yai	to make fun of
pukllay	pookh·lyai	to play (game/sport) • game • match (sport)
pukyu	pook·yoo	spring (water)
punta	poon·tah	peak (mountain)
puñuna	poo·nyoo·nah	bed
puñuy	poo·nyui	to sleep
puñuy aysay	poo·nyui ai·sai	sleepy
puqusqa	po·kos·kah	ripe
puquy	po·koy	to produce
puriq	poo·rekh	traveller
puriy	poo·ree	to hike • to walk • to travel • trip
purun llaqta	poo·roon lyahkh·tah	ruins
pusamuy	poo·sah·mui	to fetch
pusaq	poo·sahkh	guide (person)
pusay	poo·sai	to lead • to guide
puskay	poos·kai	to spin (thread)

PH

phasil	*fah·*seel	easy
phawaq	p-*hah·*wahkh	quick
phaway	p-*hah·*wai	to fly • to run • race
phawariy	p-hah·*wah·*ree	to run
phawaylla	p-hah·*wai·*lyah	fast (movement) • quickly
phiña	p-*hee·*nyah	angry
phistihay	fees·*tee·*hai	to celebrate
phukuy	p-*hoo·*kui	to play (music)
phuspuru	p-hoos·*poo·*roo	match (to light fires)

P'

p'acha	*p'ah·*chah	dress • clothes
p'achallikuy	p'ah·chah·*lyee·*kui	to wear clothes • to dress oneself
p'akisqa	p'ah·*kees·*kah	broken
p'akiy	*p'ah·*kee	to break
p'alta	*p'ahl·*tah	flat
p'inqasqa	p·en·*kahs·*kah	embarrassed
p'itay	*p'ee·*tai	to jump
p'uchukay	p·oo·*choo·*kai	to finish
p'uku	*p'oo·*koo	dish • plate
p'uti	*p'oo·*tee	key • lock

Q

-q	·kh	of
qallariy	kah·*lyah·*ree	to begin • to start
qanra	*kahn·*rah	dirty
qaparqachay	kah·pahr·*kah·*chai	to scream
qaqa	*kah·*kah	cliff • stone • rock • strong • durable
qara	*kah·*rah	leather • skin
qaray	*kah·*rai	to serve food • to feed
qasa	*kah·*sah	ice
qasay	*kah·*sai	to freeze
qasi kawsay	*kah·*see *kow·*sai	peace
qata	*kah·*tah	blanket
qatichikuy	kah·tee·*chee·*kui	to copy
qatiq	*kah·*tekh	next • following • descendant
qatiy	*kah·*tee	to follow
qaylla	*kai·*lyah	near
qayna	*kai·*nah	last
qayqa	*kai·*kah	crazy
qilla	*ke·*lyah	lazy

QUECHUA – ENGLISH DICTIONARY

qilqa	*kel*·kah	letter
qilqana	kel·*kah*·nah	pen • pencil
qilqay	*kel*·kai	to write
qincha	*ken*·chah	fence
qiru	*ke*·ro	cup (ceremonial, of the Incas)
qispi	*kes*·pee	crystal • glass • free (at liberty)
qulqisapa	kol·ke·*sah*·pah	rich
qunqay	*kon*·kai	to forget
qura	*ko*·rah	herb • plant
qurawan qampiq	ko·*rah*·wahn *kahm*·pekh	herbalist
quri	*ko*·ree	gold
qurpa	*kor*·pah	guest
qurpa wasi	*kor*·pah *wah*·see	accommodation
qurpachana	*kor*·pah·*chah*·nah	accommodation
quy	koy	to give • to pay
quya	*ko*·yah	queen
quykuy	*koy*·kui	to pay
quyllur	*koy*·lyoor	stars

QH

qhali kay	k-*hah*·lee kai	health
qhalilla	k-hah·*lee*·lyah	safe
qhampu	k-*hahm*·poo	spider
qhapaq	k-*hah*·pahkh	powerful • rich
qhapiru	k-*hah*·*pee*·roo	band
qhaqllin	k-*hahkh*·lyeen	jaw (lower)
qhari	k-*hah*·ree	man
qhatuy	k-*hah*·tui	to sell at a market
qhatu	k-*hah*·too	market
qhawachiy	k-hah·*wah*·chee	to show
qhawariy	k-hah·*wah*·ree	to look • to look after
qhaway	k-*hah*·wai	to watch • to see • care
qhilli	k-*he*·lyee	dirty
qhipapi	k-he·*pah*·pee	behind
qhipata	k-he·*pah*·tah	afterwards
qhipay	k-*he*·pai	to stay • to remain
qhusi	k-*ho*·see	blue (of eyes only)

Q'

q'aytu	k'*ai*·too	string
q'ipi	k'*e*·pee	backpack • package
q'ipiy	k'*e*·pee	to carry (on the back)
q'iyachay	k'e·*yah*·chai	to become infected
q'uchukuy	k'o·*choo*·kui	to celebrate

R

q'uncha	k'on·chah	stove
q'uñi	k'o·nyee	warm • hot
q'uñikuy	k'o·nyee·kui	to warm up
q'uñiy	k'o·nyee	to heat
q'upa	k'o·pah	garbage • rubbish
q'usmi	k'os·mee	smoke
q'usñi	k'os·nyee	smoke
q'uturichiy	k'o·too·ree·chee	to entertain

R

rakiy	rah·kee	to separate
rantiy	rahn·tee	to buy • to exchange • to barter
raphi	rah·p-hee	sheet (paper)
rap'a	rah·p'ah	page
raqch'i	rahkh·ch'ee	ceramic • pottery
raqra kunka	rahkh·rah koon·kah	hoarse
ratuchalla	rah·too·chah·lyah	fast (time)
ratulla	rah·too·lyah	quickly
rawray unquy	row·rai on·koy	temperature • fever
-rayku	·rai·koo	reason • because of
raymi	rai·mee	festival • holiday
rikch'akuq	reekh·ch'ah·kokh	lookalike • similar
rikch'aq	reekh·ch'ahkh	kind (type)
rikch'arichiy	reekh·ch'ah·ree·chee	to wake
rikch'ariy	reekh·ch'ah·ree	to wake
riki	ree·kee	of course
rikuchikuy	ree·koo·chee·kui	gift • present
rikurichiy	ree·koo·ree·chee	to exhibit
rikuy	ree·kui	to see
riluh	ree·lookh	clock • watch
rimay	ree·mai	to speak • to talk • language • word
rimaykuy	ree·mai·kui	to explain
ripuy	ree·pui	to leave • to go away
riqsichiy	rekh·see·chee	to show • to introduce (a person)
riqsinakuqmasi	rekh·see·nah·kokh·mah·see	friend
riqsisqa	rekh·sees·kah	famous
riqsiy	rekh·see	to know (people/places) • to get to know • to recognise
riy	ree	to go
rumi	roo·mee	rock • stone
runa	roo·nah	humankind • people • person • Quechua speaker

S

runakuna	roo·nah·*koo*·nah	people
rupha	roo·p·hah	fever • temperature • hot
ruphariy	roo·p·hah·ree	to feel hot (person)
ruphay	roo·p·hai	burn • sunlight
ruqya	rokh·yah	noise
ruq'tu	rokh'·too	deaf
ruruy	roo·rui	to produce
ruwana	roo·wah·nah	job
ruwanayuq	roo·wah·*nah*·yokh	busy
ruwasqa	roo·wahs·kah	done (a task)
ruway	roo·wai	to do • to make

S

saksasqa	sahkh·*sahs*·kah	full (after a meal)
saku	*sah*·koo	jacket (of a man)
samariy	sah·*mah*·ree	to breathe
samay	*sah*·mai	rest (relax) • to rest
sami	*sah*·mee	luck
samiyuq	sah·*mee*·yokh	lucky
sapa	*sah*·pah	alone • each • every
sapanka	sah·*pahn*·kah	each • every
sapaq	*sah*·pahkh	different • other
saqillay	sah·*ke*·lyai	to allow • to permit
saqiy	*sah*·kay	to leave something
saruy	*sah*·rui	to step on
sasa	*sah*·sah	hard • difficult
sat'iy	sah·t'ee	to inject • to puncture
sayachiy	sah·*yah*·chee	to stop (someone else)
sayaq	*sah*·yahkh	steep
sayarichiy	sah·yah·*ree*·chee	to build
sayay	*sah*·yai	to stop (oneself) • to stand • size • to size
sayk'usqa	sai·*k'oos*·kah	tired
saywa	*sai*·wah	border
sichus	*see*·choos	if
siki	*see*·kee	bottom (body)
silq'u	sel·k'o	signature
simi	*see*·mee	language • word • mouth • lip
sinchi	*seen*·chee	strong (person) • very
sipas	*see*·pahs	young woman
sipascha	see·*pahs*·chah	young woman
siq'inchay	se·*k'en*·chai	to draw
siqay	*se*·kai	to climb
siqsiy	sekh·see	itch (sensation)
siray	*see*·rai	to sew
sirikuy	see·*ree*·kui	to lie down

T

siriy	see·ree	to lie down
sispa	sees·pah	near • close
siwk	syookh	smooth • straight
sulpáy niy	sool·pai nee	to thank
sumaq	soo·mahkh	handsome • beautiful • nice • tasty
sumaq kawsayniyuq	soo·mahkh kow·sai·nee·yokh	honest
suni	soo·nee	long (length) • high
sunqu tupachiy	son·ko too·pah·chee	to (be in) love
suphu	soo·p·hoo	hair (body or animal)
suti	soo·tee	name
suti silq'uy	soo·tee sel·k'oy	to sign (a document)
sutichay	soo·tee·chai	to call • to name
sut'u	soo·t'oo	wet
suwakuy	soo·wah·kui	to rob
suway	soo·wai	to steal
suwirti	soo·weer·tee	luck
suyay	soo·yai	to expect • to wait
suyk'u	sui·k'oo	cup
suynay	sui·nai	sound
suyt'u	sui·t'oo	long (length) • high
suyu	soo·yoo	region

T

-ta	·tah	towards • to
taki	tah·kee	song
takiy	tah·kee	to sing
taksa	tahkh·sah	short • average
taksa puñuna	tahkh·sah poo·nyoo·nah	twin bed
takuriy	tah·koo·ree	to disturb
tanqay	tahn·kai	to push
tanta	tahn·tah	crowd • group
tapuna	tah·poo·nah	question
tapunakuy	tah·poo·nah·kui	to argue
tapuy	tah·pui	to ask (a question)
taqruy	tahkh·roy	to mix
tarikuy	tah·ree·kui	to find (something lost)
tarpuy	tahr·pui	to plant
tawa k'uchuyuq	tah·wah k'oo·choo·yokh	square (shape)
tayriyay	tai·ree·yai	to be late
timpuraq	teem·poo·rahkh	early in the afternoon
tinku	teen·koo	average • medium-sized
tinkuy	teen·kui	to meet • to meet up with
tiqsimuyu	tekh·see·moo·yoo	world • universe • space • time • Earth

tiyana	tee·*yah*·nah	chair • seat
tiyay	*tee*·yai	to live in • to sit
trawu	*trah*·woo	alcohol • liquor
trukiy	*troo*·kee	to barter • to exchange
tukay	*too*·kai	to play (music)
tukuy	*too*·kui	to finish • end • limit • everything • every • all
tullpa	*tooly*·pah	clay stove
tullu	*too*·lyoo	bone • thin • skinny
tupay	*too*·pai	to meet • to meet up with
tura	*too*·rah	friend (male friend of woman)
turi	*too*·ree	brother (of woman)
turiyay	too·*ree*·yai	to make fun of
tusuy	*too*·sui	dance • to dance
tuta	*too*·tah	evening • night • dark
tuta mikhuy	*too*·tah *mee*·k-hui	dinner
tutallamanta	too·tah·lyah *mahn*·tah	early in the morning
tutamanta mikhuna	too·tah·*mahn*·tah mee·*k*-hoo·nah	breakfast
tutaraq	too·*tah*·rahk	early in the morning
tutayay	too·*tah*·yai	to get dark
tuwalla	too·*wah*·lyah	towel

TH

thanta	t-*han*·tah	old (worn out)
thatkiy	t-*haht*·kee	to step

T'

t'aqasqa	t'ah *kahs*·kah	separated
t'aqay	t'ah·kai	to separate
t'aqsay	t'*ahkh*·sai	to wash (clothes/hair)
t'ikray	t'*eekh*·rai	to translate
t'uqu	t'*o*·ko	hole • window
t'uru	t'*oo*·roo	mud

U

uhay	*oo*·hai	drink • to drink
uhu	*oo*·hoo	cough
uhuy	*oo*·hui	to cough
ukhu	*oo*·k-hoo	deep • inside
ukhupi	oo·*k*-hoo·pee	inside • among
ukyay	*ookh*·yai	drink • to drink
uliyay	oo·*lee*·yai	baptism

uma llaqta	oo·mah *lyahkh*·tah	capital city
unay	oo·nai	delay • to delay • past
upa	oo·pah	mute • deaf
uran	oo·rahn	below
uray	oo·rai	under
urmay	oor·mai	to fall
urpi	oor·pee	dove (also an endearment)
urpu	oor·poo	jar
usa	oo·sah	lice
usqhaq	oos·k-hakh	speedy
usqhay	oos·k-hai	fast • quickly (movement)
usqhaypaq	oos·*k-hai*·pahkh	urgent
usqhayta	os·*k-hai*·tah	immediately • very soon
ususi	oo·*soo*·see	daughter (of father)
utaq	oo·tahkh	or
uyakuy	oo·*yah*·kui	to agree to • to accept
uyariy	oo·*yah*·ree	to hear • to listen • to understand

W

wahay	wah·hai	to call (shout/telephone)
wakcha	*wahkh*·chah	poor • poor person
wakcha kay	*wahkh*·chah kai	poverty
wakin	wah·keen	part • rest (remaining)
wakinkunalla	wah·keen·koo·*nah*·lyah	some (animate object)
wakiwakillan	wah·kee·wah·*kee*·lyan	some (inanimate object)
waksi	*wahkh*·see	steam
wampar	*wahm*·pahr	table
wampu	*wahm*·poo	boat
-wan	·wahn	with
wañusqa	wah·*nyoos*·kah	dead
wañuy	wah·nyui	to die
waq	wahkh	other
waqachiy	wah·*kah*·chee	to play (music)
waqay	wah·kai	to cry
waqaychay	wah·*kai*·chai	to keep
waqllichiy	wahkh·*lyee*·chee	to detour
waqlliy	*wahkh*·lyee	to detour
waqtanpi	wahkh·*tahn*·pee	beside (next to)
waqtu	*wahkh*·too	alcohol • liquor
waqyay	*wahkh*·yai	to call (shout/telephone)
waq'a	wah·k'ah	crazy
wara	wah·rah	underpants • trousers

QUECHUA – ENGLISH DICTIONARY

Quechua	Pronunciation	English
warmi	*wahr*·mee	wife • woman
warmichakuy	wahr·mee·*chah*·kui	to marry (man says)
wasi	*wah*·see	house
wasi ayllu	wah·see *ai*·lyoo	home
wasi-masi	wah·see *mah*·see	neighbour
waskha	*wahs*·k·hah	rope
wata	*wah*·tah	year • age
wata hunt'ay	wah·tah hoon·t'ai	birthday
watay	*wah*·tai	to tie
watiqmanta	wah·tekh·*mahn*·tah	again
watukuy	wah·*too*·kui	to miss (person) • to visit
waturikuy	wah·too·*ree*·kui	to visit
watuq	*wah*·tokh	fortune teller
wat'a	*wah*·t'ah	island
wawa	*wah*·wah	baby (human)
wawa qhawaq	wah·wah k·hah·wahkh	babysitter
wawtisay	wow·*tee*·sai	baptism
wayaqa	wah·*yah*·kah	bag • purse • handbag
wayk'uy	*wai*·k'ui	to cook
wayllunakuy	wai·lyoo·*nah*·kui	to fall in love
waylluy	*wai*·lyui	love • to love
waylluq	*wai*·lokh	lover
wayna	*wai*·nah	young man
wayqi	*wai*·ke	brother (of man) • friend (male friend of man)
wayq'u	*wai*·k'o	deep valley
wayra	*wai*·rah	air
wayt'ay	*wai*·t'ai	to swim
wichay	*wee*·chai	to climb • up • uphill • north
wiksayuq	weekh·*sah*·yokh	pregnant (human)
willa	*wee*·lyah	news
willachikuy	wee·lyah·*chee*·kui	message
willakuy	wee·*lyah*·kui	to confess (tell) • story
willay	*wee*·lyai	to advise • to inform • to warn
wintana	ween·*tah*·nah	window
wiñay	*wee*·nyai	to grow • age
wiñay hunt'asqa	wee·nyai hoon·t'ahs·kah	adult
wira	*wee*·rah	fat • grease
wisikilita	wee·see·kee·*lee*·tah	bicycle
wisq'ana	wees·*k'ah*·nah	lock
wisq'asqa	wees·*k'ahs*·kah	shut
wisq'ay	*wees*·k'ai	to close • to shut
wulsiku	wool·*see*·koo	pocket
wutilla	woo·*tee*·lyah	bottle
wutilla kichana	woo·*tee*·lyah kee·*chah*·nah	bottle opener

Y

yachachiy	yah·*chah*·chee	to teach • to explain
yachay	yah·chai	to learn • to know (facts) • education
yachayniyuq	yah·chai·*nee*·yokh	intelligent • wise
yananchakuy	yah·nahn·*chah*·kui	to marry • wedding
yanapay	yah·*nah*·pai	to aid • to assist • to help
yanqallan	yahn·*kah*·lyahn	free (no cost)
yapamanta	yah·pah·*mahn*·tah	again
yapa yapa	*yah*·pah *yah*·pah	often
yaqa	*yah*·kah	almost • more or less
yawarchay	yah·*wahr*·chai	to bleed
yaya	*yah*·yah	priest • God
yunka	*yoon*·kah	jungle • forest
yupay	*yoo*·pai	to count
yupaychay	yoo·*pai*·chai	to respect • to worship
yupaychay wasi	yoo·*pai*·chai *wah*·see	temple
yuray	*yoo*·rai	to plant
yuyay	*yoo*·yai	to think • to remember • thought
yuyay quy	*yoo*·yai koy	advice
yuyariy	yoo·*yah*·ree	to remember
yuyaychay	yoo·*yai*·chai	to advise • to counsel
yuyaysapa	yoo·yai·*sah*·pah	intelligent • wise
yuyayukuy	yoo·yah·*yoo*·kui	to realise

INDEX

SUSTAINABLE TRAVEL

As the climate change debate heats up, the matter of sustainability becomes an important part of the travel vernacular. In practical terms, this means assessing our impact on the environment and local cultures and economies – and acting to make that impact as positive as possible. Here are some basic phrases to get you on your way …

COMMUNICATION & CULTURAL DIFFERENCES

I'd like to learn some of your local dialects.

nyoo·*kah*·kah *mai*·kahn	Ñuqaqa maykan
kahn·pahkh *lyahk*·tah	qanpaq llakta
ree·mai·koo·*nah*·tah	rimaykunata
yah·chah·hoo·*nah*·yahn	yachajunayan.

Would you like me to teach you some English?

ah·shah een·*glee*·stah nyoo·kah	¿Asha inglista ñuqa
yah·cha·chee·*chee*·nah *kahn*·tah	yachachichina qanta
moo·nahn·*kee*·choo?	munankichu?

Is this a local or national custom?

kai·kah *nyow*·pah kow·*sah*·nah	¿Kayqa ñawpa kawsana
kai·*mahn*·*tah*·choo kai	kaymantachu kay
mah·mah·lyahk·*tah*·choo kah·pahn?	mamallaktachu kapan?

COMMUNITY BENEFIT & INVOLVEMENT

What sorts of issues is this community facing?

kai ai·lyoo·koo·*nah*·kah ee·mah	¿Kay ayllukunaqa ima
lah·yah har·kah·koo·*nah*·tah	laya jarkakunata
cheen·pah·*nah*·joon?	chinpanajun?

media control	wee·*lyai*·koo·nah·*mahn*·tah *kah*·mai	willaykuna-manta kamay
political unrest	ah·*poo* kah·*mah*·yookh *mah*·nah kah·*see*·lyah *tee*·ahkh	apu kamayuq mana kasilla tiaq

| poor living conditions | *wahk*·chah kow·sai·*koo*·nah | waqcha kawsaykuna |
| religious conflict | pah·chah·kah· mahk·*mahn*·tah mah·kah·*nah*·kui | pachaka- makmanta makanakuy |

I'd like to volunteer my skills.

| *nyoo*·kah yah·chah·nah·*koo*·nah koo·*yah*·nah moo·nah·*yah*·nahn | Ñuqa yachanakuna kuyana munayanan. |

Are there any volunteer programs available in the area?

| *ee*·mah mah·*kee*·tah koo·*yah*·nah yoo·yah·*nah*·kui *kahn*·pahkh lyahk·*tah*·pee tee·*ahn*·choo? | ¿Ima makita kuyana yuyanakuy kanpaq llaktapi tianchu? |

ENVIRONMENT

Where can I recycle this?

| mai·*pee*·tahkh *kai*·tah koo·teekh moo·*shook*·pee roo·rah·nah·*koo*·nee? | ¿Maypitaq kayta kutiq mushuqpi ruranakuni? |

TRANSPORT

Can we get there by public transport?

| nyoo·kahn·*cheek*·kah too·*kui*·pahkh ahn·tah·*wahn*·pee chai·mahn cha·yah·*nah*·tah oo·shah·neen·*cheek*·choo? | ¿Ñuqanchikqa tukuypaq antawanpi chayman chayanata ushaninchikchu? |

Can we get there by bicycle?

| nyoo·kahn·*cheek*·kah peesh·kee·lee·*too*·pee chai·mahn cha·yah·*nah*·tah oo·shah·neen·*cheek*·choo? | ¿Ñuqanchikqa pishkilitupi chayman chayanata ushaninchikchu? |

I'd prefer to walk there.

| nyoo·*kah*·kah poo·ree·*ee*·mahn chai·mahn | Ñuqaqa puriiman chayman. |

ACCOMMODATION

I'd like to stay at a locally run hotel.

nyoo·*kah*·kah shookh kai	*Ñuqaqa shuq kay*
lyahk·tah *roo*·nah kah·*mah*·cheek	*llakta runa kamachik*
poo·*nyoo*·nah wah·*see*·pee	*puñuna wasipi*
poo·nyoo·*nah*·yahn	*puñunayan.*

Can I turn the air conditioning off and open the window?

wai·rah·*chee*·tah	*¿Wayrachita*
wah·nyoo·chee·*shah*·choo	*wañuchishachu*
kah·wah·nah·*tah*·peesh	*kawanatapish*
pahs·kahn·*gah*·pahkh	*paskangapaq*
oo·shah·nee·choo?	*ushanichu?*

Are there any ecolodges here?

kai lyahk·tah·*mahn*·tah	*¿Kay llaktamanta*
wah·*see*·pee poo·nyoon·*gah*·pahkh	*wasipi puñungapaq*
tee·ahn?	*tian?*

There's no need to change my sheets.

nyoo·kah pah·*chah*·tah *mah*·nah	*Ñuqa pachata mana*
moo·*dahn*·kee sah·*kee*·lyah	*mudanki sakilla.*

SHOPPING

Where can I buy locally produced souvenirs?

mai·*pee*·tahkh *ee*·mah	*¿Maypitaq ima*
mah·kee·roo·rahsh·*kah*·tah kai	*makirurashqata kay*
lyahk·*tah*·pee rahn·deen·*gah*·pahkh	*llaktapi randingapaq*
oo·*shah*·nee?	*ushani?*

Is this made from animal skins?

kai·kah *chee*·tah kah·rah·*koo*·nah	*¿Kayqa chita karakuna*
roo·*rahsh*·kah *kahn*·choo?	*rurashqa kanchu?*

Which forests are these products sourced from?

mai·hahn sah·chah·*mahn*·tah kai	*¿Mayjan sachamanta kay*
mah·kee·roo·*rahsh*·kah	*makirurashqa*
ah·pah·*moon*·kee?	*apamunki?*

FOOD

Do you sell …?	kahn·choo hah·too·koon·kee …?	¿Qanchu jatukunki …?
locally	kai lyahk·tah·pee	kay llaktapi
produced	mee·koo·nah	mikuna
food	roo·rahsh·kah·tah	rurashqata
organic	kai aly·pah·pee	kay allpapi
produce	lyook·sheesh·kah·koo·nah	llukshish qakuna

Can you tell me what traditional foods I should try?

kahn·kah oo·shan·kee·choo
mai·hahn kai·mahn·tah
mee·koo·nah·koo·nah·tah nyoo·kah
mah·lyeen·gah·pahkh moo·nah·nee?

¿Qanqa ushankichu
mayjan kaymanta
mikunakunata ñuqa
mallingapaq munani?

SIGHTSEEING

Does your company …?	kahn·pahkh rahn·dee·nah·kah·too·nah …?	¿Qanpaq randinakatuna …?
donate money to charity	kooly·kee·tah kah·rai wahk·chah·koo·nah·tah kah·rah·pai·choo	kullkita karay waqchakunata karapaychu
hire local guides	kai lyahk·tah·mahn·tah poo·shahk·koo·nah meen·gah·gree	kay llaktamanta pushaqkuna mingagri
visit local businesses	ree·koo·green·kee·choo rahn·dee·nah·kah·too·nah wah·see·koo·nah·mahn kai lyahk·tah·pee	rikugrinkichu randinakatuna wasikunaman kay llaktapi

Are cultural tours available?

ree·cheek poo·reen·gah·pahkh
tee·ahn·choo?

¿Richik puringapaq
tianchu?

NUMBERS

0	*ch'oo*·sahkh	ch'usaq
1	hokh	huq
2	*ees*·kai	iskay
3	*keen*·sah	kinsa
4	*tah*·wah	tawa
5	*pees*·kah	pisqa
6	*sokh*·tah	suqta
7	*kahn*·chees	qanchis
8	*poo*·sakh	pusaq
9	*ees*·kon	isqun
10	*choon*·kah	chunka

EMERGENCIES

It's an emergency!	*seen*·chee os·k-hai*pahkh*·mee!	¡Sinchi usq-haypaqmi!
Could you please help?	ah·*lyee*·choo yah ·nah·pah·wahn ·kee·koo·*mahn*·choo?	¿Allichu ya napa-wan kikuman chu?
I'm lost.	*cheen*·kai cheen·*kai*·lyah poo·ree·*koo*·nee	Chinkay chinkaylla purikuni.